Maid for the Family

By John Silver

About this Book

Ten fascinating tales of enforced maid (and other) service. In the title story a crossdressing son begins by borrowing the maid's uniform, ends up as well-strapped uniformed junior maid for his family, then is passed on to his younger sister, who finally has him shipped off to bordello slavery In South America.

In *Forgone Conclusion* a nephew is captivated by a ladies rubber cape, is thoroughly humiliated by his girl cousins by being forced to dress publicly as a little girl, then is tricked into being a maid for them and his aunt.

In *Instant Cuckold* a wife takes the neighbour as a lover, he becomes a slave maid to them both.

In *A Job Opportunity* casual help sorting ladies' clothes has him trying them on, is caught and 'persuaded' by the husband to become a slave maid and his concubine.

In *Loo Lady the* Company Accountant is transformed into just that, after being caught out in fraud.

In *Neighbourhood Watch* a flirt seduces her neighbour; both her and hubby end up as his slaves.

In *Superior Secretary* a lady subdues stepdaughter by harnessing her as a ponygirl.

In *Tenancy Agreement* the young landlord becomes maid to the black tenant's extended family.

In *The Colonial Convert* the former master dresses up his maid, then dresses in her clothes, ends up enslaved by her family, then on his return to Blighty is recruited as a shemale slave before sliding right down the scale to toilet cleaner.

Fascinating stories of male to shemale transformation and what can happen afterwards, by way of the joys and tribulations, the pride and humiliation, pleasure and pain.

Copyright Notice

Table of Contents

Maid for the Family

I realise now that my family was rather strange. Dad seemed to be in one shady business after another. Mum was a lady who liked the good things in life and needed a man who would supply them. On the face of it they suited each other, but my early memories were of them quarrelling all the time.

When I was about fifteen years old they sort-of split up. They did not get divorced but Mum lived in one house and Dad lived about 5 miles away. I went with Mum and Susan, my sister who was 4 years older than me, went with Dad.

There never seemed to be a shortage of money. When there was a business dinner or conference they usually went together and quite often Dad would bring her home and stay the night. It was a very cosy arrangement.

Mum seemed to spend most of her time shopping or having tea or cocktails with her friends. We had Mrs Holmes as cook/housekeeper and two girls we called May and Joy as housemaids. They were from some Far Eastern country and it was only much later I found out that Dad had bought them both from their parents on one of his business trips and, as they were in the country as servants, they could not leave. Mum treated them like slaves and Mrs Holmes was very strict with them. However I never heard them complain and they seemed to expect such treatment.

It was just a week after my sixteenth birthday when I had, what I would call, my first real sexual experience. I was in the big broom cupboard in the kitchen looking for something when the kitchen door swung open with a bang and May stumbled into the room. I froze and peeped through the crack of the partly open door. Mrs Holmes followed May in and said, "Right my girl. I'll teach you to cheek your Mistress. Fetch the strap!"

"Sorry, Mrs Holmes," May said in her sing-sing voice but she went over to one of the kitchen drawers and took out what I now know was a two-fingered tawse.

I could not see Mrs Holmes from where I was but I saw May go back to her and then Mrs Holmes said, "Now get over that table!"

I could just see May bending over the end of the kitchen table and Mrs Holmes hand laid down the tawse on the table. Then I saw her hands as she pulled May's dress and petticoats over her back and took her knickers down. As I struggled to get my now rampant penis out of my trousers and not lose sight of the table, Mrs Holmes picked up the tawse. I pushed the door just a little and I saw the first stroke come down across poor May's buttocks leaving a red stripe. My penis jerked a little and I pulled a hanky from my pocket with my left hand as I held my cock in my right. Whack! A second stroke came down then a third. Six strokes left May's buttocks glowing red and me with a hanky full of cum.

"Put the strap away and get back to your work." Mrs Holmes said.

"Yes, Mrs Holmes." May said in a rather tearful voice. I watched as she pulled up her knickers and tidied herself then after closing the drawer on the strap, scurried out of the kitchen.

"You can come out now Master Jack." Mrs Holmes said.

I did not move. The door swung wide open and I was standing there, cock in one hand and hanky in the other.

Mrs Holmes was smiling "I see you enjoyed that."

"Yes Mrs Holmes." I said.

"Apart from sneaking about in my kitchen don't you think it is rather naughty to enjoy yourself watching someone else's discomfort?"

"Yes, Mrs Holmes."

"What do you think I should do about it then?"

"I don't know Mrs Holmes."

"Maybe you should be punished?"

It was that moment I realised why I was so excited. Not in seeing May get hurt, but imagining myself in her position.

"Yes Mrs Holmes."

"Yes what, boy?"

That stopped me for a second. I was not sure what I was getting into. She bent over and looked me straight in the eyes, "Yes what boy?" She said again.

"Err! Yes please, Mrs Holmes."

"Come out of there, boy!"

I crept out, trying to put my still half-stiff penis away. As I did so, Mrs Holmes went over to a chair and sat down.

"Over my knee, boy, and don't worry about that thing. I've seen plenty of them."

I went over and stood beside her.

"Well get over then, boy."

I hesitated because a vivid picture came into my head. Mrs Holmes pulling my skirts pulled up and my knickers down before punishment.

"Well, boy." Mrs Holmes said, "What are you waiting for?"

"Err you took May's skirts up and knickers down first." I said.

"Yes but you're not wearing skirts or knickers are you? I can take your trousers and pants down if you like."

Maybe it was the resigned look on my face or the tone in my voice as I said. "No, that's all right Mrs Holmes," because she burst out laughing.

"Oh I get it. *You want to be a girlie.* Well there's no time for all that now, but drop your pants anyway and bend over."

The word *girlie* started to stiffen me up again, so I struggled a bit obeying the order.

Mrs Holmes was grinning as she watched me, and she said "Maybe it would be better to have you in skirts next time."

She had been about to start preparing dinner so she was wearing a plastic apron, which was cold on my bare legs, but felt lovely pressed against my penis.

Whack! Her work-hardened hand came down across my right buttock. I gasped with the pain and then whack! It came down across my left one.

Six on each cheek I got but, as I was to find out later, they were not as hard as she could do them if she wanted to.

"Up you get!" She said at last.

I stood up, my eyes brimming with tears. She looked down at her apron, now stained with my semen.

"You had better wipe that clean." She said.

"Sorry Mrs Holmes." I replied. Fortunately I had another hanky in my other pocket and quickly wiped up my mess.

"You know that is not the sort of dirty thing a nice girl does." She said "You'll have to be punished again for that and this time we will have you dressed properly. Go and get yourself ready for dinner."

"Yes Mrs Holmes and thank you for my punishment." I said and turned to leave.

"I should think so too. Now don't mention of this to anybody else."

"Of course not, Mrs Holmes."

For the next few days I was in a state of constant excitement expecting that any time Mrs Holmes would order me into the kitchen or better still into the staff quarters which were in the converted stables. Once there my imagination ran riot and my hand worked overtime but Mrs Holmes behaved as though nothing had happened.

It must have been a month later. Mum was away at a conference with Dad and had taken Joy to act as her personal maid. Mrs Holmes had gone out for the day so there was only May and I in the house.

What I did not know was that when May had had her punishment that day Joy had been waiting in the hallway to comfort her and the two girls had heard everything through the kitchen door. I finished breakfast as May came into the room: she grinned at me. "You want be a girl?" She asked.

I was startled. I did, but did not know what to say.

May took my silence as agreement and went on, "You come to kitchen. May make you a girl. Yes?"

She walked to the kitchen, with me following her. As I stepped inside I saw one of her uniforms hanging on a cupboard door. On the table were laid out bra, panties, suspender belt, some black stockings and a white slip.

"You like?" she said waving her hand towards the uniform.

"Oh, yes please." I gasped out.

She grinned, "May dress you as maid, but you promise to do as May says or smack."

"Oh yes." I breathed out.

"Undress now." She said, and I could not wait. Within minutes I was standing naked and my clothes were draped over the chair.

She started with the bra and suspender belt, and then when I stepped into the matching panties she pulled them up with some difficulty over my rampant cock.

"I deal with that later." she said, "You finish dressing now."

She watched as I pulled the stockings up and clipped them to my suspenders. I was already thinking of them as my suspenders. Then I put on the slip and the blue polycotton overall dress, which buttoned up the front. Then I donned the disappointingly plain-bibbed apron and the elasticised kitchen-maid's cap.

The shoes were a problem, but I had white trainers so they did not look too bad.

"Can't I have a prettier apron May?" I asked.

"You skivvy now. You wear what you are told."

Her words were as good as having a frilly apron and I made a little curtsey and said, "Yes May."

"It, 'Yes Mistress'," she said, "now we deal with nasty bulge." She flicked her hand at my very stiff penis, which was pushing the front of my dress out. "Stand by sink and face it. Take knickers down."

I did as ordered and waited, expecting to be milked by May's little hand.

She came over and with one hand she picked up my skirts and the other slapped a frozen bag of peas into the join of my penis to balls. My erection collapsed. The next minutes she was tying a ribbon round the end of my limp member then she passed it under my crotch and reaching under my dress fastened it to the back of my suspender belt so tight that it pulled my penis between my legs with my balls pressed up into my groin.

I was gasping in pain but May was quite calm.

"Pull knickers up girl, and we find you work."

May did just that. She had me cleaning, dusting, ironing, scrubbing floors etc. One job after another and whilst I was working she was either supervising or once she decided I was doing it correctly she disappeared into the staff lounge and was watching television. The first time she came back from the lounge I was brushing the stairs and she was carrying the tawse.

Whack! She caught me one across my buttocks.

"Hurry up girl." She said "There is lots to do yet and I want my lunch shortly."

"Yes Mistress." I replied as she walked away.

I served her lunch at the dining room table, but I never got any until she had finished and she said as I stood in the corner of the dining room ready to serve.

"You may clear and wash up girl. You may have the scraps. Make sure you eat them all up."

It was nearly 6 o'clock when she said, "You may get changed now girl. Mrs Holmes will be back shortly. Put your clothes in the wash."

I curtsied and said, "Yes Mistress. Thank you Mistress for wonderful day."

"Ah!" she said, "May forgot. Let me see. One cup marked with lipstick, a blouse to re-iron, and the lounge to re-dust. Six strokes. Yes?"

She brought the tawse from behind her back.

I did not reply, just lifted my skirts and bent over the table.

May pulled my knickers down. My penis was still fastened backwards between my legs but it was trying to stiffen. May's hand went between my legs and pulled it back even more.

Then she said, "Close legs tight."

As I did so it trapped my penis between my legs and May let go. She brushed the tip with her fingers and with a little giggle she said, "Make nice target."

The first stroke landed across my left buttock and the tips of the tawse caught the edge of my right buttock. I gasped and May took aim again. This time she was more accurate and the tips of the tawse caught the end of my penis. I squealed and jumped up.

"Get down!" May shouted "And don't move again."

Eyes watering I got down again. My partial erection had subsided. May unfastened the ribbon from my suspender belt and to my horror she pulled it tighter.

"Close legs." She said and when I did so she retied the ribbon and went over to one of the kitchen drawers. A moment later I felt her passing another length of ribbon round my thighs. She did this twice and tied it.

"Naughty girl move must be fastened." She said.

Again she flicked the exposed tip of my penis and gave another chuckle then stepping back she swung the tawse. This time she was slightly low so my penis escaped but the next blow was on target and it took all my self-control to stay still. The next two were accurate as well and by the time she released me my penis was stinging and my arse was red and sore.

"You get changed now." She said "And from now on you obey May, yes?"

"Yes, thank you May."

My cock was almost too sore to masturbate that night but I managed. Four times!

May served dinner that night and every time she walked behind my mother she grinned at me. Once she bent over my chair and said, "You quite comfortable Master Jack? Shall I bring you cushion?"

I blushed and Mum said, "What was that about?"

"Oh I fell over in the yard today on my bottom and May thought it was funny."

Mum gave a little laugh. "I expect it was."

I was looking forward to when I could be May's maid again but several weeks went by before anything happened. That is apart from me sneaking knickers and bras out to the laundry basket to try on.

One Monday evening Mrs Holmes was talking to Mum at dinner when Mum said, "I've got the ladies coming for cocktails on Friday and I can't think of anything to amuse them. Have you got any ideas Eileen?"

It had become something of a competition with the ladies to have some amusing twist to the afternoon. That was how I first became involved when she had me in my best suit reciting a poem. I was petted and pampered, made to sit on several ladies' knees while they fed me with grapes and put a casual hand on my thigh to feel if I was stiff. Which I was by the time I was off the first knee. After that I was expected to attend every time the party was in our house.

Mrs Holmes looked thoughtful for a moment and said, "Well Madam what about, instead of having May or Joy to serve the ladies, we put Master Jack in a maid's uniform and have him serve."

Mum looked startled and then laughed, "Oh Eileen I don't think he would do that. Would you Jack?"

I blushed and said, "Well Mum, if it will help I don't mind."

"What a good boy. What about his uniform and would he be able to do it nicely?"

"Well Madam we have three days, If he was to work with me as a housemaid for those three days he would get used to wearing girl's clothes and I could teach him how to serve."

"Yes I suppose so, but he would still need a uniform."

"Oh he could borrow one of the girls uniforms for the training and I could take him into town on Wednesday and buy him a nice parlour-maid's outfit. Oh and some undies of course."

"Brilliant Eileen, but I think we could both take him. I am not going to miss that."

She turned to me, "All right Jack, in the morning you report to Mrs Holmes to work as a maid for the rest of the week. Is that clear?"

"Yes Mum."

I could see the look of satisfaction on Mrs Holmes face then she said, "I will find him a uniform tonight Madam and some undies and he can get dressed straight away in the morning."

"Good idea Eileen. That's settled. The ladies will be surprised."

Mrs Holmes went to go back to the kitchen and then stopped as though an idea had just come to her. However I knew this was part of the plan from the start.

"Just one thing Madam."

"Yes Eileen?"

"Discipline, Madam."

"What about it?"

"Well you know how I discipline the staff?"

"Of course."

"What about Master Jack, when he is part of the staff?"

"Ah I see. Well I suppose if he is one of your staff, then you will have to use the same system."

"Thank you Madam."

With that she left and Mum broke into a laugh. When she calmed down she said, "Oh Jack, you are in trouble."

"Am I Mum?"

"Oh yes my lad. Mrs Holmes keeps a nice leather strap in a kitchen drawer to use when the girls are lazy or cheeky and I have just given her permission to use it on you. I suggest you try and be on your best behaviour for the next few days." With that she got up. "I have to meet your father with some buyers from South America in an hour. Be a good boy. Whoops, sorry I mean, 'girl'." With that, she swept out of the door still chuckling.

I went into the lounge to watch a film. After about an hour Mrs Holmes came in.

"Right Master Jack, come to your room. I want to try your uniform on you." She said and went out again.

I could not wait; I was right on her heels and once in the room she was standing there with a bra and suspender belt in her hand. On the bed was the same uniform that May had made me wear, except it had a tabard instead of the apron. Well I knew of course it would be, but I was still disappointed that it was not a black and white parlour maid's one and I knew that the girls wore tabards when they were going to do the dirty jobs. I knew then what sort of treatment I was going to get.

"Get stripped off." Mrs Holmes ordered. I quickly obeyed.

She put the suspender belt round my waist, showed me how to put the bra on backwards then twist it round and put my arms through the straps and then she handed me a pair of white support knickers to put on. They were quite tight and a bit of struggle but she made no attempt to help me.

"You know your Mum gave me permission to use the strap don't you?" she asked.

"Yes, Mrs Holmes."

"And you remember that you are due a punishment already?"

"Yes, Mrs Holmes."

"I bet you did not think you would be getting it in front of May and Joy did you?"

"No, Mrs Holmes."

"Well that is what is going to happen tomorrow, but right now put this petticoat on and I will show you how to do your make-up."

The make-up was the miniMum, foundation, powder, lipstick and blusher.

"That will do to work in," she said "I will do you a really elaborate job on Friday. Now get your dress and tabard on and we will see how you look."

She watched as I did so and then said, "Whoops we forgot your stockings but you can put them on can't you."

"I think so, Mrs Holmes."

"You can wear your white trainers to work in and we will get you some shoes when we get your uniform on Wednesday."

"Thank you, Mrs Holmes."

"Right; in the morning I want you in the kitchen at 7.30 dressed like this. If you are late it is one stroke of the strap per minute or part of the minute and one stroke for every item of clothing I am not satisfied with, including make-up. Is that clear girl?

"Yes Mrs Holmes."

"You can go and watch television again but I suggest you keep the uniform on. It will help you get used to it."

"Yes, Mrs Holmes. Thank you."

With that she left the room.

The first thing I had to do was to rush to the bathroom to deal with a growing tightness in my knickers.

The next morning I was dressed, made up and in the kitchen by 7.20. Mrs Holmes was already there. She looked me up and down.

"Not bad," she said, "we'll check your undies when I punish you."

My knickers started to tighten and at that moment May and Joy came in from the servants' quarters.

They stopped and stared. I had assumed that Mrs Holmes had told them but she had not.

"It's Master Jack." May said.

"No!" Mrs Holmes said, "This is now Janie our new trainee maid. Well at least until the weekend. She will be working with you and while I will supervise, it is up to you girls to see she does her work properly and report to me any faults or disobedience. Is that clear?"

"Yes, Mrs Holmes." They replied together and they were both grinning.

"The first task this morning is to punish Janie. She knows what for. Mary you prepare her, and Joy get the strap."

Suddenly I was grabbed, pulled over to the end of the table and bent over. Mary pulled up my skirts and with some difficulty pulled down my knickers. I felt her hand go to my penis, I assume to pull it through, but it was rock hard and she just stood up and said, "Legs together girl." And laughed.

Mrs Holmes laughed as well. "Now girls" she said, "Janie is going to get six of the best and you are to watch, so you know she is just a servant like you."

"Yes, Mrs Holmes." They both replied.

Whack! The first blow came and my arse was on fire. I started to get up.

"Stay there miss, or I will have you tied down and it will be a dozen."

I got back down and gritted my teeth.

"Whack." The second one was on the other cheek and just as painful, as were the last four.

"Right girl, stand up and tidy yourself and don't let me have any trouble from you this week."

I painfully stood up and pulled up my knickers, which was a lot easier as my erection had subsidised. I smoothed my skirts and turned to Mrs Holmes.

She looked at my tear-stained eyes and said, "You curtsey and thank me now, girl."

That started to get me stiff again as I gave a clumsy curtsey and said, "Thank you for my punishment, Mrs Holmes."

"Hum! We will have to practise that curtsey before Friday." She turned to my two fellow maids and said, "Janie will be serving at the cocktail party on Friday."

The grins got wider. "I see Mrs Holmes." May said, "Will she be practising serving before then?"

"Oh yes, she can serve us at meal times and she can serve Madam on Thursday evening in her new uniform to make sure she is ready to attend to Madam's guests."

That was a busy day. I cleaned toilets, made beds, washed up and when Mum came to see how Mrs Holmes was getting on I was scrubbing the floor in the utility room. When Mum saw me she gave a little laugh and turned to Mrs Holmes.

"Well I see you've got things well in hand Eileen. She will be ready for Friday won't she?"

"Oh yes Madam. I am going to have her serve dinner to you on Thursday in her new uniform, so you can check."

"Very good. I'll leave you to it."

I slept like a log that night and I only just made it to the kitchen in time. This time all the staff was present and Mrs Holmes had a piece of paper in her hand.

"Ah Janie. Just in time," she said, "I've got a list of yesterday's faults here. One broken glass, part of the utility room had to be redone, two attempts at making Madam's bed. Four strokes; bend over the table."

"Please, Mrs Holmes. It was an accident with the glass and it was the first time I had made a bed."

"I know Janie, but you were careless with the utility room, that is two strokes. I'll let you off one stroke each on the other matters because of the circumstances but as you have chosen to argue with me I will put them back. Six strokes now and if you are not over that table with your knickers down in 5 seconds it will be eight."

I quickly obeyed and once again ended up with a red stinging bottom. As I straightened my clothing Mrs Holmes said, "I am not being cruel Janie. You have to learn your job and to be servile and obedient very quickly. This is the best and easiest way. Now get on with the work girls. I have to take Janie for her new uniform this afternoon."

The morning seemed to drag as the two maids ordered me about and watched as I did their work. When I was time for a break and their lunchtime I had to serve at the table with Mrs Holmes holding the strap ready to whack me if I got anything wrong. At last it was time. Mrs Holmes produced a pink plastic raincoat with a hood for me to wear and we met Mum in the hall. She had her fur coat on and when she saw me she smiled. "Pity you haven't got a nicer coat to wear Janie." She said "If I decide to keep you as a girl I will get you one."

My slack penis jumped into life at that. Mum was thinking of keeping me as a girl. I could hardly believe it.

Mrs Holmes drove the car, Mum sat in the back like a princess and I sat beside Mrs Holmes.

"Don't forget to open the car door for Madam when we arrive," she told me.

"Yes, Mrs Holmes." I said.

The shop was where Mrs Holmes bought the girls uniforms and the sales lady greeted her like an old friend and Mrs Holmes introduced her to Mum then said, "Madam has taken this young man on to be trained as a maid servant." Mrs Holmes told her. We have some working uniforms for him as you can see but he has to serve at a cocktail party for Madam's friends so we need something more formal."

The lady looked me up and down, "A young man you say? Well apart from his short hair I would not have known. Do you want something feminine?"

"Oh yes, very feminine."

"Well, come over to the formal department ladies, and we will see what we can find."

Up to then it was my most embarrassing experience. The word somehow got round the shop that a boy was being fitted with a girl's uniform and several giggling ladies came by as I stepped in and out of the changing cubicle with different dresses on, so Mum and Mrs Holmes could see how they looked on me. Finally they decided on a dress in a satin material with tiny pearl buttons down the front. It was calf-length and it had a lace collar and cuffs on the three quarter sleeves. They chose a waist-length apron with lace edging and a black French maid's cap with ribbons down the back to my waist. I saw myself in the mirror and nearly fainted with excitement.

"We will need some suitable shoes for him." Mum said.

"Yes Madam, they do have a shoe department. I'm sure they can help us."

And so it proved. Black patent leather with a two-inch heel and ankle straps.

Eventually we were on our way back home.

"You know," Mum said, "I enjoyed that and I'm quite looking forward to seeing Janie serving the ladies in that lovely uniform.

"Me too, Madam." Mrs Holmes said

I could not wait for Friday, but first there was a lot of housework to do, two more beatings and lots of, "Yes, Mrs Holmes," or "Yes, Miss May," or "Yes, Miss Joy," as I obeyed a long and seemingly unending stream of orders.

Thursday evening went like a dream. I served Mum her dinner and, unlike the other girls, she made me wait by the wall as she ate. She asked me how I liked being a maidservant and I told her that, apart from the beatings, it was quite nice.

"So Mrs Holmes has beaten you, has she?"

"Yes Madam, every day for any mistakes I made the previous day."

"Oh now, I think that's wrong," Mum said, "Fetch Mrs Holmes in to see me."

'Now she is going to get it,' I thought as I hurried to obey. When Mrs Holmes came, in I went back to my place.

"Mrs Holmes Janie tells me that you have punished her with the strap every day for mistakes made the day before."

"Yes Madam, you said it would be in order for me to discipline her."

"Oh yes Mrs Holmes, of course, it is but I think when you are correcting mistakes in this way the punishment should be carried out as near to the time of the error as possible. Now I know that may be inconvenient, but I think it is important."

"If you say so Madam. I will do my best to see to that."

"Thank you, Mrs Holmes. Tell me, how many strokes do you give for a mistake?"

"One if I think it is a genuine error, and two if I think it is carelessness."

"Hum, if it is for training purposes and I assume it is."

"Yes Madam, it is."

"Then an error is an error no matter if it is careless or not. I think three strokes for every mistake and add one stroke each time the error is repeated."

"Yes Madam, and thank you for your advice."

"You're welcome, Eileen. You may go."

When Mrs Holmes had left the room Mum turned to me and said: "Well my girl, I think you are going to learn your new duties fast or have a very sore bottom."

"Yes Madam." I replied with some feeling.

The next day I was thinking so much with anticipation of what was going to happen to me that afternoon that I had nine strokes of the strap before lunch. Then after lunch had been cleared May and Mrs Holmes took me into the servants' lounge and started to prepare me for my afternoon duties. The make-up alone took nearly an hour, but eventually I was allowed to look at myself in the long mirror. There I saw the prettiest parlour maid I had ever seen. My poor penis was struggling to expand under the tight corset that had been put on me to give me my feminine figure.

"Right my girl. Let's take you to Madam." Mrs Holmes said and she marched out of the door and I followed, mincing along on my high heels.

Mum was delighted. "That is just lovely Eileen," she said, "I wonder what Fiona Jessup-Harrington will offer now?"

"Oh yes, Madam. Has she made an offer then?"

"She certainly has. After the first time Jack was at the party and then she doubled it a few weeks later."

Although I was conscious of my position as a maid I could not resist asking, "Excuse me Madam. My I ask a question?"

Mum turned and looked at me for a second or two although deciding if a maid should be allowed to ask questions.

"Yes Janie."

"Please Madam what did Mrs Jessup-Harrington make an offer for?"

Mum and Mrs Holmes laughed, "For you silly. She wants to buy you."

"Buy me Madam. What for?"

"Oh I don't know. Train you and keep you chained to her bed I suppose."

"But that would be slavery and that's illegal."

Again both ladies laughed, "Yes, my little naive one, but it still goes on. Look at May and Joy. Your father bought them."

"I know Madam, but he was only paying a sort of dowry to their families."

"Call it what you like my dear. But what about the 50 or so dowries he has paid since then. Where are those girls? Certainly not working here, are they?"

"I don't know Madam. Where are they?"

"Flat on their backs in some South American bordello with their legs wide open I shouldn't wonder." she said and both ladies laughed again.

I was a bit shocked "But that's slave trading."

"Yes and his recent trips to Eastern Europe have been quite profitable as well. There is a nice market opening up in some parts of Africa. Some of those oil-rich locals think it is fashionable to have a couple of white house-slaves."

"Really Madam?" Mrs Holmes said.

"Yes and they take both boys and girls. Well the South Americans will take the odd pretty boy as well of course, but any white boy will sell in Africa."

She laughed again and then looked at me, "So you had better be a good girl hadn't you Janie or you may find yourself curtsying to some black Mistress. Give her three strokes of the strap for insolence Eileen. After the party! I don't want her squirming about in the corner all afternoon."

I wasn't squirming as I waited in the hall for the first of Madam's guests to arrive. I was shaking with fear.

The make-up was good and the first two ladies' comments were to note that Madam had got a pretty new maid and compliment me on my uniform. However Fiona Jessup-Harrington was not fooled. I knew her quite well. She was the one who had me on her knee and fondled me much more than the others. She was slim, well more thin really, and in the late forties or early fifties. Even thought the general idea was exciting I did not fancy being chained to her bed at all.

She looked at me for a few seconds and then a broad grin broke out all over her heavily made-up face.

"Its Jack isn't it?"

"Janie now, Madam." I said with a curtsey.

"Very pretty, Janie. Take my coat. Are you serving the refreshments later?"

"Yes Madam, and I am to entertain as well, but I have not been told how."

"Don't worry your pretty little head about that. I think we will manage to amuse ourselves with you."

With that she went off to the lounge chuckling.

I minced about, serving the ladies with hands going up my skirts and feeling my bottom all the time. Mum was congratulated on my appearance and I sat on several knees. Eventually I had to lift my skirts for the ladies to examine my undies and see how I was restrained.

"Are you going to keep him as a maid, Jean?" one lady asked my Mum.

"Oh I am thinking about it. He is 17 now and he's not got a job yet. Bob would take him into the business I suppose but Alice, our daughter you know, is well into running it and I am afraid she would make it difficult for Jack. It would be nice for him to have something to occupy him."

I was standing by the wall behind Mum waiting to serve, when she said this and I started to get excited again, which was rather uncomfortable. I was worn out by the time they started to leave. I helped them on with their coats and got lots of pats on the cheek and several £5 and £10 notes pushed down my bra. Mrs Jessup-Harrington smiled at me. "I will be seeing you again soon Janie." She said and swept out.

Mum was delighted with the party.

"I went so well Eileen." She said.

"Did that Mrs Jessup-Harrington make an offer then?"

"I'll say. She doubled her last one and when I refused she threatened me. The cheeky cat."

"Threatened you, Madam?"

"Yes she said that Jack would soon be 18 one day and able to please himself. She said she would have some of the prettiest uniforms possible made for him and them offer him a job as her parlour maid. Then she said she would make the uniforms so pretty he would not be able to refuse."

"What did you say Madam?"

"I told her that Jack did not really like wearing girls clothes and only did it because I insisted. So it would not do her any good."

She turned to me. I was still standing by the coat stand waiting for orders.

"So you're quite safe, Janie. All you have to do is refuse."

"Yes Madam." I said, but I was not as confident as she clearly was. How pretty were the uniforms going to be I wondered?

The next day I got up and dressed in my ordinary clothes. Somehow things felt a bit empty. I went down to breakfast and Mum was already there.

"Ah Jack I so pleased with you. You made a lovely maid."

"Thank you Mum."

"However I forgot that Mrs Holmes was to punish you after the party."

"Oh Mum you're not going to make me have the punishment, are you?"

"I always keep my word. However there is also the question of what we are going to do with you. Mrs Holmes has suggested that we could give May and Joy one day off a week and you could take the place of which ever girl was off and carry out her duties."

My heart gave a leap but I said, "Do I have to, Mum?"

"I think it is a good idea. It will give you something to do until we decide what your future is going to be. Also you can help out when Mrs Holmes is not here. I will put May in charge and you can do her work."

I then sealed my own fate, "Will I have to wear the same uniform as the girls?" I asked.

I could see Mum relax as my reply had made it clear that I was not going to object.

"Of course you will, which is another thing. We have bought your uniforms, they might as well get used."

At that moment May came in with my breakfast.

"Now May, " Mum said, "please tell Mrs Holmes that Master Jack will be helping with the housework when one of you has a day off. She can go ahead and plan his schedule starting Monday. He will probably need an extra dress and a couple more aprons and tabards."

"Yes Madam." May said with a curtsey, "And thank you for the days off."

"That is all right May, just make sure you continue to deserve them."

The first thing that happened Monday morning when I reported for duty, was Mrs Holmes carried out Mum's orders and I got three strokes hard across my bare buttocks.

As I pulled my knickers up and my dress down Mrs Holmes lifted my chin and looked into my tear stained eyes and said, "Now let that be a lesson to you young Janie and be more respectful to your elders and betters."

I worked as a housemaid at least three days a week. I often worked more, if one of the girls was ill or Mrs Holmes decided to take her away for a long weekend. When I was on duty everybody in the house and visitors treated me like a junior housemaid, which made me feel both safe and content. About six weeks later two of Mum's friends came to visit. I was not on duty that day, so I did not serve them. That evening at dinner Mum said, "Ann and Sylvia came over today."

"Yes Mum I saw them."

"Why did you not come and have tea with us?"

"I thought it might be private."

"Well yes it was sort of, but you could have come, as it concerns you."

"I suppose they want to buy me?"

Mum laughed, "No my dear they want to borrow you and I said they could."

"What for?"

"It's a surprise. It's Ann's turn to do the cocktail party and she wants to use you."

I perked up at that, " What, as a maid?"

"They said not, but they would not tell me. It is a surprise of course. It is on Friday and Sylvia is going to collect you early Friday morning."

"What shall I wear?"

"She said it did not matter, but be ready at 8 o'clock."

"Yes Mum."

"You know, this being a girl half the week is doing you a world of good. You are so polite now. I might make you wear dresses all the time." But she was grinning.

Sharp at eight Sylvia turned up in her car. I was wearing jeans and tee shirt but she made no comment. To my surprise we drove to her house where Ann was waiting.

"Hallo Janie." She said leading my straight up the stairs. "We are preparing you here because we want it to be a proper surprise and some of those cows are not above bribing my staff to find out what I am going to do."

She took me into a very feminine bedroom

"What are you going to do with me?" I asked.

"Well look." She said.

On the wardrobe door was the most gorgeous party frock. Mainly pink but trimmed with red roses and masses of white frills. It looked like the sort of dress a nine-year-old girl would wear, only big enough for me.

"You are going to join the party as one of the girls."

It would have been a humiliating dress for a 17-year-old girl to wear, so it was doubly humiliating for me. I pointed this out to the ladies and they laughed.

"We are glad you think that Janie, because that is exactly the effect we want to have on you. We want you as a soppy little sissy. You will have a dolly to carry with a copy of this dress." She picked up a doll from the dressing table and she was right; the dress was an exact copy.

This was too much. "Oh no I can't do that, it's too much."

The ladies stood and looked at me for a moment.

"You can and you will," Ann said, "we know Mrs Holmes uses the strap on you if you are disobedient, and we will do the same thing. We have a strap and my gardener is here today. He will hold you if I tell him to and we will beat you until you agree to do as you are told. Your Mum said we could punish you as we saw fit, if you did not co-operate. Of course she did not know what we intended to do with you."

I certainly did not fancy being beaten in front of the gardener so I said, "Yes Madam Ann."

She smiled, "Good, we are going to get you ready now so you get used to the clothes. Get stripped."

I'm not sure which was the most humiliating garment. It may have been the stiff petticoat that made my skirts stick out, the dress itself or the long split-crotch pantaloons that ended at my ankles with lots of frills just above my patent leather Mary Jane shoes. Not that it mattered at all; there was a lot more humiliation to come.

It was an hour before the ladies were satisfied. Then they took me to the hall and let me look in the long mirror. I knew they had put a wig on me, but only then I saw it had two plaits with ribbons on the ends matching my dress. I looked again at the doll, which Ann was carrying and saw it had the same plaits.

Ann said, "Now stand there, Janie and don't move, "here, hold your doll."

I was totally subdued by now and just said, "Yes Madam Ann." And took the doll.

"I am going home now," she went on, "to get ready for the party. Madam Sylvia will bring you, so you be a good girl while she gets ready."

Another hour went by, as I stood where I was told. Sylvia had a housekeeper and a live-in maid and they seemed to spend a lot of time going back and forward across the hall grinning at me. Eventually Sylvia came back in a lovely cocktail dress followed by her maid carrying some clothing.

"Here Janie." She said holding out a piece of scarlet material trimmed with white fur. "This is your dolly's cape, put it on her."

Not being practised it took me a few minutes but the two ladies just stood and watched me patiently. Finally the doll was ready with the fur-trimmed hood over its head, its hands through the arm slots and the tiny buttons down the front fastened.

"Put the doll down Janie." I put it on the hallstand.

"Janie's cape please, Maria."

The maid was grinning as she handed me a cape identical to the one I had just put on the doll.

"Put it on Janie."

I slipped the cape over my shoulders and putting my arms through the arm slots fastened the buttons then, without being told, pulled the hood over my head.

Sylvia seemed quite pleased.

"Pick up your doll." She ordered, as her maid helped her on with her fur coat.

"Come on, we will be just in time," she said and headed for the door, which her maid had hurried to open.

I followed, but to my surprise we did not go towards the garage but headed straight down the path to the front gate.

"Please Madam Sylvia, are we not going in the car?"

Sylvia smiled down at me. "It's not far through the park Janie, and it's a nice day for a walk. Besides." she went on smiling even more, "it would be a pity to not let that nice cape have an airing wouldn't it?"

What could I say or do? Shaking with a mixture of fear and excitement I followed Sylvia out of the gate, the few yards down the road and then turn into the park gates.

As it was early afternoon most children would be at school so the park was fairly empty. There was however some ladies pushing prams some of which were quite interested in a young girl dressed in such an old fashioned way.

Two ladies were walking the other way and one said so Sylvia as we approached, "What a pretty outfit. Is she going to a party?"

We stopped and the ladies examined me as Sylvia replied, "That's right. Would you like to see her dress?"

"Yes please."

As Sylvia took the doll off me the ladies noticed it.

"Oh look Mary." One of them said "Her doll is dressed the same."

"Undo your cape, Janie," Sylvia ordered, "show the ladies your pretty dress."

In a sort of trance I did as ordered and there were 'oohs' and 'aahs' as they fingered the material.

"Well we must get on ladies. Do up your cape, Janie."

I quickly did up the buttons and as I did so one of the ladies said, "Thank you for showing up my dear. I must say she is a very pretty little girl."

Sylvia handed me back the doll.

"Thank you but its is not she, it's a he, as he makes such a very pretty girl."

I nearly died of embarrassment as the two ladies broke into peals of laughter.

"Well, he is going to be quite a hit at the party I'm sure." One of them said and they walked on still chuckling.

We also walked on and I said, "Why did you tell them I was a boy, Madam Sylvia?"

She grinned, "Oh I like to humiliate young men like you and any boy who allows himself to be used as a girl deserves everything he gets."

A few minutes later we arrived at Ann's house. I was escorted into the lounge still in my cape and carrying the doll. There were peals of laughter from the expectant ladies.

I could feel my blushing cheeks as I looked round the familiar faces. To my horror there was Mum sitting on the couch, with Susan sitting beside her, clearly enjoying every minute of my humiliation.

When the ladies had calmed down Madam Ann said, "Take your dolly's cape off, Janie."

In a sort of trance I did that and there were several comments about the doll's pretty dress.

"Put the dolly and cape on the chair Janie."

I did that.

"Take your cape off girl."

There was a clapping of hands and expressions of appreciation as I revealed my pretty dress and petticoats. I was inspected and passed round so everyone could see my ultra feminine outfit. Eventually I was passed to Susan.

"Well Jack, you do make a pretty girl," she said, "I wish now you stayed with Dad and I. I would have had my own personal maid by now."

Mum, who had been sitting next to her grinning, chimed in, "Well my dear, you are 21 next month and I think I will give you Joy to be your maid. I have trained her well."

"Thank you mother. But what will you do?"

"I think I will train May to take Joy's place."

"Mrs Holmes won't be pleased losing an experienced maid for a big part of the day."

"Oh I don't think that will be a problem. She can have Janie instead."

My mother and sister broke into peals of laughter at my expression. I could not think of anything to say and at that moment Madam Ann tapped me on the shoulder.

"Janie," she said, "go into the kitchen. My maid is about to serve the refreshments. You can help her."

"Yes Madam Ann." I replied and as I started towards the door I heard Susan say, "What an obedient and pretty little girl that is."

Madam Ann's maid was waiting for me. She held up a pinny, which was white with pink frills round the armholes and the bottom hem. It matched my dress beautifully.

"Come on miss," she said, "get this pinny on."

I slipped my arms in and she spun me round so she could fasten the buttons at the back.

"I'll take the sandwiches and you take the cakes," she said.

"Yes Miss."

"I understand your mother has had you trained as a housemaid."

"Yes Miss."

"When I first heard I could not understand that, but know I see what a prissy little girlie boy you are, I think it is probably a good idea."

The rest of the afternoon seemed to go like lightning. After the first round of refreshments the maid was dismissed and I took over. Eventually I helped the ladies on with their coats until only Mum, Susan and I were left. I had to dress my doll and put my own cape on while the ladies watched me.

"Come on then Janie and Susan." Mum said, "Let's go home."

We stepped out of the front door. There was only Madam Ann's car in the drive.

"Where's the car Mum?" I asked.

"Oh we came by taxi but it's a nice afternoon, so I think we will walk home. It's only a mile or so."

I could not believe it. It was late afternoon and all the children would be out of school. Ladies would be coming back from shopping and there was no park to walk through. The way back was via a housing estate and down a main road. However, there was no choice. I was going to walk home between two elegantly dressed ladies, looking like a very sissy version of Little Red Riding Hood and carrying a dolly.

I had one last try, "please Mum let me wait here and bring the car for me."

"Oh no Janie. Susan suggested this and I would not like to disappoint her. Besides if you're going to be a full time housemaid, and you are, humiliation will be very good for you."

Humiliating it was too. I was stared at, pointed at, laughed at and called too. A couple of sixth-formers in school uniform called to Mum.

"Has she been to a fancy dress party then?"

It was Susan who laughed and answered. "Well sort of girls, but it's not a she it's a he."

Before we reached out gate four more girls had joined the other two. Just outside the house they caught up with us.

"Can we have a good look at the nancy boy, Miss?" they asked

Mum was just going in the gate and I was following her but Susan grabbed my arm and swung me round.

"Help yourself ladies." She said.

Mum stopped, "Bring Janie inside when your friends have finished, please Susan." She said.

"Yes Mum." Susan replied then she turned to the six girls now surrounding me "Go on open his cape and have a look at his undies if you like."

While they looked Susan explained that I was her brother, but I was to be trained as a housemaid and kept in girl's clothes full time. The girls all agreed it was a good idea and one asked if I could come to her 17th birthday party in a couple of months time.

"You will have to ask my mother," Susan said, "He is going to be her maid."

Then to my relief she took me inside.

It all happened very quickly. Joy went to live with Dad and Susan the following Monday and I was handed over to Mrs Holmes. We were in the lounge and I was dressed in my working maid's uniform.

"Now Eileen, Janie is to be treated just the same as you treated May and Joy," Mum told her, "she is now a junior housemaid and that is all she is."

Mrs Holmes grabbed me by the ear. "Don't you worry, Madam. I will have her trained and obedient in no time. Come on girl, let's put you to work."

I was marched out of the room to my new life, which at the time I thought was going to go on until I was 21. I knew that Susan had been made a director at 21 and Dad had plans to do the same for me. So I could enjoy being a girl for few years knowing that it would come to an end.

It was about six weeks later. Mum and Dad had been invited to stay with a prospective customer in Africa. She had left May at home, as the man assured her that he had several slaves trained as ladies maids. Mrs Holmes simply took over from Mum. May was her housekeeper and I was the maid. It was hard work but Mrs Holmes made a good lady of the house and May was a strict Mistress.

It was Susan who brought the news. Mum and Dad had been out on the man's yacht for a few days. The authorities were not sure if it was pirates, a rival businessman or someone the man had upset, but what they did know was the yacht was attacked and sunk with everyone aboard. There were no survivors

"Just carry on." Susan said, "The lawyers and I will take care of everything."

We did as she said. Mrs Holmes moved into the master bedroom and May and I continued to work as her servants. Then one day Susan arrived. First she took some took some pictures of me naked, in my undies and in uniform. I asked her what they were for but she said. "You just do as you are told girl."

Then she had us all in the dining room.

"I am selling both houses," she said, "and I am buying a large house with lots of ground and stables. Mrs Watson", who was Dad's housekeeper, "is retiring so would you like to be my housekeeper at the new house Mrs Holmes? You can bring May with you."

"That would be good Miss Susan, but what about Janie here?"

"I'll take care of Janie. Now a lot of the furniture will go to the new place but some pieces I have sold to some buyers in the states. I will mark them and let you know when the removal men will be here."

The day finally came and Susan arrived in her car shortly after the removal van. The men loaded it and Mrs Holmes put her own and May's luggage in Mum's car. The Susan and I watched as the van pulled away followed by Mrs Holmes.

As they left a smaller van came down the drive.

"Good, the boys are here." Susan said, "You help them as much as possible Janie."

"Yes, Miss Susan."

The men opened the van doors and the first thing they did was to lift a cage down and place in on the lawn. Then we started to carry out some valuable antiques which Mum had collected and carefully put them in the van. When it was all loaded Susan said, "Put the girl in the cage."

Before I could react the two men grabbed me, Susan swung the cage door open and I was pushed in. There was a click and the door was locked.

"What's happening Susan?" I said.

She lent on the cage and grinned, "I've sold you." She said and smiled even more. "Unfortunately for you I have a problem with the will. You will become a joint director with me on your 21st birthday. I did try and dissuade Dad from doing that but he would not change it and unfortunately for you that sealed your fate."

"What are you going to do?" I asked now quite scared.

"I have already done it. We have an agent in South America and I sent him those pictures. He contacted a bordello who we have supplied before. They specialise in different sorts of whores and they just loved those pictures of you; I am getting myself a very good price for you."

"No, please Susan." I said "I'll refuse the directorship and you can use me as your personal maid."

"Susan smiled again, "No, I don't think so my little sissy brother and don't worry about being rescued or anything. The lads here have shipped loads of girls, and a few boys. In a week or so you will be lying on your tummy in a tarty outfit with a nice big cock up your sissy arse. I do so hope you enjoy it."

"But I'm your brother Susan. You can't do this."

"Oh I can but you are right. Blood is thicker that water so I have made some arrangements."

"What arrangements?"

"I have offered to pay towards the operation for you and the hormones."

"Operation! What operation?"

She laughed "Oh what a naïve little girl you are. Let's just say that afterwards your knickers won't be so tight afterwards but your bra will be."

I went white, "No, please, Susan."

"Sorry little brother, but it may turn out for the best in the end."

"Why?"

"You see this is a high class place and after three or four years they reckon their whores are getting a bit worn so they sell them on. I have first refusal on you."

"So you will buy me back?"

"Maybe, if I have managed to sort out the directorship problem. In any case, by the time you have spent a few years as a woman being fucked by a dozen or so men every day I don't think you will give me lot of trouble. I mean everyone knows that you practically volunteered to be Mum's maidservant. I'll just say you arranged to be a prostitute yourself and I found out where you were and rescued you. I mean who are they going to believe?"

She was right and what could I say but, "Yes Susan. Thank you Susan. Will I be able to work for you as a maid?"

She shrugged "Oh I don't know maid, general skivvy, pony girl, guard dog. It's not important but I will make sure you are put to good use."

"Please Susan, promise to buy me back."

"Ah little slave, that will depend on you. I will find out just how co-operative and obedient you have been then make up my mind."

Just then the two men came over.

"Ready Miss?"

Susan nodded and I was swung up into the van.

Actually Susan was more thoughtful than I expected. I am writing this in the mate's cabin on a cargo boat. He has had strict orders to look after me and make sure I don t come to any harm and I am kept a virgin.

I keep the cabin tidy and he said oral sex does not affect my virginity so I do that for him. I am only allowed on deck wrapped in my cloak and when he is there. He asked me to write this and he told me that I am to go straight to the clinic to be feminised when we dock. That will be in about an hour so I had better see to my makeup and get my things together. Goodbye.

Foregone Conclusion

Really David did not stand a chance. There was, for a start, no male influence in his life. He was brought up by Alice, his mother, and for the first few years with the aid of his Aunt.

Aunty Thelma was a few years older than David's mother and she had two daughters. David's Mum usually did what her elder sister said and David took it for granted that what Aunty Thelma said went. When the first significant incident occurred David thought that his Aunt had been kind to him. It was only much later he realised that she resented his mother having a son and that her actions were more likely to have been motivated by this. Not that it mattered, as it was too late by then and it would probably made little difference to David had he known at the start.

David began his journey into this present life style when he was sixteen. Aunty Thelma had moved to the south coast and started a ladies dress shop. She had wanted Alice to go with her but she was settled into a promising career in a local electronics firm, and for once stood her ground.

Thelma had come to London on business with the girls and on the Saturday, while she was visiting suppliers, Alice took the girls shopping. As long as he could remember David had liked to try on girl's clothes but what he saw when his cousins first arrived made him more excited than he could ever remember. Capes were fashionable at the time and Shirley, the eldest, was wearing a dark green rubberised satin rain cape with a hood and matching booties. David just had to try it and the opportunity was handed to him on a plate. It was not raining or cold so the girls went off with no coats.

At first it was just the cape but then the booties. That did not look right with his trousers so it was a dress and some tights and he swished up and down in front of the hall mirror before going to his room to satisfy himself into a towel. To this day he still wonders if his Aunty knew or guessed. He was lucky with his timing. Everything was back in place twenty minutes before she walked in the door. Maybe he had not put something away properly but nothing was said apart from his Aunty ordering him to make her tea.

What made David wonder about Aunty knowing was what happened about a year later. David and his Mum were staying in Thelma's new house for a long weekend. After David and his younger cousin, Susan, had washed up Aunty said.

"We always go out for a walk after Sunday dinner."

"But it's raining." Alice objected.

"All the more reason. We have had a super new line in very smart plastic raincoats in and we have all got one so we can try them out. You've got a raincoat haven't you?"

"Yes but I forgot to bring David's, so he will have to stay home."

"Nonsense. We can fix him up. Get your coats on girls and I'll fetch one for David."

David could not believe his eyes. He blushed and was struck dumb and Thelma carried in the green rain cape in one hand the boots in the other.

Alice laughed, "He'll look like a girl in that."

Aunty Thelma smirked and said, "So what, nobody will know and I'm sure David won't mind."

It was then that David thought she knew about the incident in London, because she came towards him holding out the booties and said with a broad grin on her face, "You won't mind at all will you David?"

"Err no Aunty." Was all he could say, and took the booties then sat down to change into them.

"The girls are wearing jeans the same as you so that won't matter. Put the boots and the cape on then, come into the hall."

With that she turned and left him, followed by her sister who was smiling faintly.

David was very glad that the cape was full because by the time he had it on and buttoned up his jeans were bulging at the crotch. He went into the hall where the ladies were pulling up their hoods on some nice white plastic raincoats with pretty blue trimmings.

"Now put your hood up David." His mother said and when he did so she pulled the on the draw stings and arranged it nicely to frame his face.

It was the most exciting walk David had ever had. They went over the cliff path, which was deserted, but then they went down a steep path and back along the beach into the town. By this time it had stopped raining and the streets were quite busy.

Of course Thelma knew a lot of people and kept stopping to talk.

He actually came in his pants when she introduced Alice to one of her customers as her sister and David as her niece Diana.

All the way back home the ladies were chuckling about that.

"You are terrible, Thelma." Alice said "What if David had had to speak to her?"

Thelma laughed, "Well he didn't and I thought his little curtsey was just right."

Thelma had Susan and David prepare tea.

"Mind you put an apron on, Diana." She said with a chuckle and Susan insisted that he did.

At five o'clock they set off back to London. As they got in the car Thelma handed David a big carrier bag and kissed him.

"A little present for you, my dear. Don't open it until you get home."

David could hardly wait; as soon as they dropped the bags in the hall he emptied the bag on the couch. It was the booties and the green rain cape with a little note.

"For Diana, a very pretty girl," Alice read and shook her head.

"That Thelma. She's a real comedian. Well you had better hang it in your wardrobe. You never know, it may come in useful.

David was too excited to even speak as he carried his prize upstairs. As he slipped the cape over his shoulders he resolved that there was nothing he would not do for his Aunty.

Alice's career moved up a notch when Robert arrived. An American corporation had bought out the company and Robert had been transferred over as managing director. He immediately appointed Alice as his PA.

She had to spend a week in America. This coincided with the college break and Susan and David's 18th birthdays, which were only a week apart.

"That's a pity," Thelma said on the phone, "but David can come and stay for the week while you're away. Tell him not to forget his rain cape."

David arrived on the Saturday morning with his cape and booties as instructed.

"One of the hotels is going to do the party David, his aunty said, "You have brought your costume?"

"Oh yes, is it a pool party?"

"Not your swimming costume you dummy. Your fancy dress costume."

"What you didn't say anything about fancy dress."

"I'm sure I did. Oh dear what are we going to do."

"What about my Tinkerbelle outfit mother?" Susan said.

"Now that's an idea. Susan was Tinkerbelle in the drama group pantomime last Christmas David. Let's see if the costume will fit you."

"Oh now Aunty I couldn't everyone will think I'm a poof."

"Now don't be silly David. It could be the winning costume and nobody will think you're a poof, as you put it, because you will look like a girl."

"No, please Aunty. I couldn't."

She looked at him frowning, "In this house I'm the boss and you will do as you're told, my lad. Get the costume, Susan."

David could not believe his eyes. It was a pink dress with a satin bodice decorated with white and pale pink flowers and two tiny wings on the back. The skirt was like a ballerina's tutu. It stood out almost horizontally supported by three stiff net petticoats. He had to wear pink tights and ballet shoes and over the tights went some very frilly pink knickers, which matched his bodice.

Once Thelma was satisfied the dress would fit it was removed, and David was handed a pink body to put on. No allowance was made for his modesty. Thelma and the girls stood around and watched as he tried to fasten the poppers on the crotch over his growing erection.

"He needs a panti-girdle mother," Shirley said in a matter of fact tone.

"You're right dear. Have you got one that will fit?"

"Susan has. She got one for her birthday."

"Oh Mum I haven't even worn it," Susan said.

"I'll get you another my darling. Now go and get it, then we can get his hair done."

Fifteen minutes later, a tight panti-girdle, a pink body and a pair of pink tights contained David's genitals, as he sat in a chair with a nylon cape over his shoulders. Thelma and Shirley applied rollers and setting lotion to his hair. When they finished Thelma said, "That will take time to set. You can sit in the lounge and watch television whilst we have our baths."

An hour later they came back wrapped in dressing gowns.

"Come on Diana, let's get your curlers out and do your make-up

Once this was done the dress went back on and Thelma carefully fasted the imitation diamond tiara in the middle of David's new curls. They all stood back and looked.

"Oh yes, Diana. You are going to be the belle of the ball. Now go into the hall."

As he went into the hall David saw that there was a black velvet evening cloak hanging on the hallstand. Thelma picked it up and draped it over his shoulders, and having fastened the clasp at the neck she draped the hood over his head.

"Lovely!" she said, "Now you just stand by the wall and look pretty while we get our costumes on."

David stood there getting more and more excited at the prospect of going to the party as a girl. Eventually they were off in Thelma's car. When they arrived at the hotel, waiting for them was a tall man in his middle forties looking very smart in a dinner jacket. He kissed Thelma and the girls in turn then looked at David.

"David, this is Mr Jack Wilson. He is my business partner and he is judging the fancy dress competition, so you had better be nice to him. Jack this is my nephew David or Diana for tonight."

"Very pretty too. Hallo Diana. I am reserving the first dance with you after the competition. When do you want the judging Thelma?"

"Oh fairly soon, before we get well into the dancing and some of the costumes will get spoilt."

Half and hour later David was lined up with the other entries and they all paraded in front of Jack. David won first prize. There were two to choose from a lovely make-up case with make-up in it and a very nice gentlemen's weekend case all fitted out.

Jack picked up the make-up case and handed it to David. Then he claimed his dance.

David could not believe it. Here he was dressed as a girl and dancing with a mature and experienced man who was clearly enjoying himself. After the first few minutes the floor was full of dancers and Jack gradually steered his partner through the throng out through the patio doors. Eventually he stopped dancing by the garden steps and said, "Well my dear Diana. It's a very nice night, shall we go for a walk in the garden?"

Without waiting for the bemused David to reply, he took a firm grip on his arm and led him down the steps. Very soon they were out of sight of the hotel and deep in the trees and bushes. Suddenly they came into a clearing and on one side was a summerhouse. In the moonlight David could see it was open one side, with chairs and a table. Jack led him over to it.

"Why have you brought me here?" David said.

Jack laughed, "You little tease. You know why we are here, come on."

He put his arms round David and the next moment he was kissing him full on the lips.

For a moment David responded. He was, after all, trying to think of himself as a girl. Then realised how dangerous this was and he started to pull back.

"No please Mr Wilson. I'm not really a girl."

But Jack just tightened his grip and with a grim tone in his voice he said, "Oh yes you are and you're a teasing bitch. Just a minute." He let go of David but then took a firm grip on his arm. With his other hand he picked up a cushion of one of the chairs and dropped it between them. "Now down on your knees bitch." He put his hands on David's shoulders and forced him down. Holding him there with one hand he unzipped his trousers and while David watched, as thought in a trance, he fumbled around in his crotch.

"No!" he said suddenly "This is your job. Get my cock out, you slut."

Jack had chosen the right words. David felt like a girl and a slut and he felt submissive. Suddenly Jack was his Master and his hands went to the open zip, as Jack's hand came back to his shoulders to hold him firm.

The next moment a large semi-erect cock was dangling in front of David's face. He stared at it without moving.

"Suck it, you tart." Jack ordered and David took it in one had and brought the end to his lips. Jack gripped the back of his head and pushed his now rampant cock into David's mouth.

"Come on, suck."

David did as ordered and was rewarded with a gush of semen into his throat.

"Swallow it." Jack ordered and David did.

A few seconds later, it was all over. Jack put his cock away and zipped himself up. Then he pulled David to his feet, picked up the cushion and put it on the chair.

"Hallo, what have we here?" Thelma's voice came from the bushes. David did not know how much she had seen.

They both stood looking at her.

"You randy old sod, Jack. Anything in skirts." Thelma said laughing.

Jack grinned, "Well, she's a sexy little thing."

"She certainly is. How would you like to see her regularly?"

"How do you mean?"

"Oh never mind, but I've got plans for this little minx which may be good for us all. Come on we had better get back to the party."

Of course, David wanted to know what these plans were, but he had not time to ask then. When they got back into the ballroom there was a queue of boys waiting to dance with him and he was treated as a real girl for the rest of the evening.

On the way back home he was at last able to ask.

"What plans have you got for me Aunty?"

Thelma laughed, "Never you mind Diana. Lets just say you have talents, which could be very useful to me. You leave college at the end of next term don't you?"

David confirmed he did and had to be content with that.

The next morning he slept late. He did not wake up until Susan shook him and said, "Come on lazy bones. Your clothes are on that chair. Hurry up, there is work to do."

David climbed out of bed and straight into the shower. As he was drying himself he looked at the chair. On it was some girl's undies and over the back was pretty cotton summer dress. He looked round. His case was gone and all his boy's clothes. The only thing in his wardrobe was his rain cape. He shrugged his shoulders. After last night it did not seem to matter what clothes he wore. He was soon dressed and sitting at the dressing table brushing his still curly hair. He prize was on the dressing table as well and he looked at it for a moment then got up and went downstairs.

The ladies were having breakfast in the dining room.

"There you are Diana," his Aunty said, "sit down and have some breakfast. I want to talk to you."

David did that. Then he said, "My clothes are all gone, Aunty."

"Susan I didn't tell you to take David's things, just to put the dress and undies in there."

"Well it thought he might not get the idea, Mum."

Thelma sighed, "We just thought that you seemed to have enjoyed wearing girl's clothes so much yesterday, that you might like to try again today."

"Well, yes Aunty. Thank you. It is a nice dress."

"Well now you are dressed you might as well be Diana for the day. I'll show you how to do your make-up after breakfast."

David had a lovely day. He had to help with the chores. He wore a pretty apron for that and after lunch the girls took him down to the beach. He could not go swimming, as he did not have a girl's bathing suit so he sat by the girl's things and looked after them.

The next morning he woke up to the sound of his Aunt's voice calling goodbye.

"The girls are coming to the shop with me David," she said, "you can look after yourself can't you?"

"Yes Aunty."

"I've left you a little list of jobs in the kitchen. You can come to the shop later if you like."

"Yes Aunty."

David got out of bed. Nothing had been said about his clothes last night and he did not know where they were, so he had no choice but to put his dress on again. This time he managed the make-up and his hair was still quite curly. He looked at himself in the hall mirror. To his prejudiced eye he looked like a pretty girl. He slipped an apron on and had breakfast. The list of chores was not long or difficult and by lunchtime David had completed them. After lunch he looked at the bright sunshine and sighed. He would have liked to go out in his cape but it would have looked silly, so he spent a pleasant afternoon trying on lots of his cousin's clothes.

David really enjoyed the rest of his week. He did some housework for his Aunt in a dress and apron, a couple of days he went to the shop and helped sort out and iron new stock and one day when there was a summer shower he did manage to go for a short walk in his cape.

That week filled his thoughts during his final term at college. This did not mean he was unaware of the mother's growing involvement with her boss. It was also clear to David that Robert did not like him much. Not that he was rude just rather cold and withdrawn when David was around. It was not a surprise but a bit of a shock when his mother announced to him that she was going to marry Robert.

"We are going to live in the states," she said, "you can come with us, of course."

Oh yes, thought David, and just how long would that last?

"Oh, I don't know Mum. Let me think about it."

David did very little thinking. The next day his mother answered the phone and then handed it to him. It was Aunty Thelma, "Now David your Mum's off to the States."

"Yes Aunty."

"I assume you don't want to go?"

"Not really, Aunty."

"Good! Now your cape must be getting a bit small for you. Am I right?"

David was surprised at this but it was true. "Well yes, Aunty."

"How would you like a new one?"

"Well, yes."

"If you come and live with me, I'll buy you one."

"Thank you Aunty, but I need a job and what can I do down there."

"You let me worry about that. Tell your Mum you are coming to live here."

The wedding arrangements were quickly made. Several times David imagined that his Mum wanted him to be a bridesmaid and he looked in the bridal shop and imagined which dress he would wear. Of course she didn't and his cousins were bridesmaids, so at least David had some hope of trying the dresses on later.

The happy couple set of for the States the day after the wedding and David went with his Aunty to start his new life.

As they drove home Thelma said, "I've got your new cape at home."

The girls giggled.

"Now girls, this is serious. It's about David's future."

"What's my future, Aunty?"

"Just wait until we get home. We've got a surprise for you."

David was agog with excitement. His Aunty had surprised him many times in the past; some surprises more pleasant than others.

Once back at the house David carried his bag in.

"Leave the bag there for the moment and come with me," his Aunt said.

David followed her upstairs and then up the narrow stairs that lead to the attic. When the attic door opened he was surprised to see that the rubbish had been cleared out, a dormer window fitted and it was quite a pleasant little bedroom.

"Look in the wardrobe," his Aunty said smiling at him.

David opened it and hanging in front of him was lovely pale blue rain cape with a hood. He started to erect immediately.

"Take it out," Aunty said and he lifted it down.

Behind it was a blue striped dress with a white-bibbed apron hanging over the top of it. David hardly noticed it as he started to undo the buttons on the cape.

"Not yet!" his Aunt said sharply "If you want to wear that you have to earn it. Now lay it on your bed."

"What do I have to do Aunty?"

"See the dress and apron."

"Yes."

That's your morning uniform. You will find others in there and undies and aprons in the drawers. Did you bring your make-up case?"

"Yes, Aunty."

"Good, the girls will bring it up with your toilet bag. Everything else will be scrapped including those clothes you have on."

"But why, Aunty."

Thelma went up to him and took him by the arms, "You, my dear," she said slowly "will be our new maid. From now on you will wear nothing but maid's uniforms and girls undies and we will train you as our full-time live in maidservant."

David was a stiff as a poker. His hand went down to his crotch.

Thelma saw the action and smiled, "That will be locked up so there will be none of that nonsense, and it's Madam to you from now on."

David stood and looked at his Aunty, then at the uniform and then at the cape on his bed. Of course, he thought, this is what I am destined for. There is nothing else to do.

Slowly he sank so his knees. As he did so the girls came in carrying his make-up case.

"Thank you Madam," he said "I hope I can be a good maidservant for you and your daughters."

Thelma stepped back, "Oh don't worry, Diana, you will I promise you."

She turned and saw her girls waiting by the door.

"All right girls. You can get her ready to serve tea."

And then walked through the door without a backward glance, quite content that she had found a permanent solution to her servant problem.

Instant Cuckold

Brian never found out if Jill had deliberately pruned the large bush between their back garden and Jeff's, or whether it was just a bit of over-enthusiasm. All he knew for certain, was that it was a hot sunny summer that Saturday morning, as he finished dressing in the bedroom. Jill was starting to make the bed when she looked out of the window.

"Oh my!" She said, "That is gorgeous."

Brian came over to the window.

The day before you could not see anything of Jeff's patio because of the thick high hedge, but now, through the thinned out branches, you could see Jeff's bronzed body stretched out on a sun bed. Despite the fact that he was in his late 40's, about 15 years older than them, he had a good firm figure, but what had made Jill comment was not his body but that he was naked and sporting a very presentable erection which he was gently stroking. Brian could see he was reading a magazine, which he assumed, must be pornographic.

Brian pressed his rapidly stiffening penis against his wife's buttocks as he gripped her round the waist, "I bet you would like a bit of that." He said.

Jill looked up into his face and felt his growing excitement, "Right my lad." She said as she pushed him back "If that's your attitude we'll see."

She pulled the strings of her pretty frilly apron undone and lifted it over her head. Then she turned and put the apron over Brian's head. For that moment Brian was stunned and as he stood there Jill walked round the back of him and tied the apron in position.

"You can make the bed and tidy the bedroom. I am going to sunbathe." And she started to walk to the door. As she went through it she said over her shoulder, "Don't forget to do the washing up from last night and you can clean the kitchen while you're at it."

Brian was a stiff as a poker by now, "Yes Mistress," he said

"I'm not your Mistress." Jill called back "It's 'Madam' to you."

In state of excitement Brain started on his tasks. Just as he finished the bed he heard the metal legs of their sun bed scraping on the patio. He looked out of the window and saw Jill lay face down on the bed and cover herself across the hips with a towel. Other than that she was naked.

Brian was about to go downstairs when she called, "Jeff. Have you got some sun cream?"

"Yes Jill. Do want to borrow some?"

"Yes please can you bring it round?"

"Of course."

Brian watched frozen to the spot and in a few moments Jeff appeared in a towelling robe carrying the sun cream.

Jill looked round and smiled, "Put some on my back there's a dear." She said.

"Of course." And Jeff went do her and started to do just that. He rubbed it into her shoulders and slowly worked his way down her back until he got to the towel. Jill reached behind her a flicked the towel off without a word. Jeff carried on rubbing the cream into her buttocks and legs until he reached her feet.

"Do you want the front done?" he asked.

Brian could only stand at the bedroom window and watch as Jill replied, "Oh yes please." And she turned over.

The next moment his lovely wife was having cream rubbed into her beautiful breasts by his next-door neighbour in his full sight. The picture and the humiliation of knowing that Jill would know he was watching had him too excited to move as Jeff worked his way down her body and eventually between her legs. This stage lasted a few minutes and he carried on down her legs.

When he reached her feet she said, "That was lovely, Jeff. If you get the other sun bed out I'll return the compliment."

Jeff put the cream down on the little table by Jill's bed and went to the shed returning with a bed. He opened it and put it by the small table. While he was doing this Jill stood up, "I bet that lazy husband of mine is idling. Brian!" she called. "Get yourself out here now!"

Brian came out of his trance and rushed downstairs forgetting he was wearing a frilly apron. As he came out on to the patio Jeff was just about to take off his robe but he stopped, wondering what was going to happen when Brian saw his naked wife. However his grim expression broke into a broad smile when he saw Brian's apron.

"Have you cleared last nights dishes and washed up?" Jill demanded.

"Err, not yet Madam," was all Brian could say.

"Why not, just get on with it but first bring me a cold lemonade. Would you like one Jeff?"

"Oh yes please, if it is not too much trouble."

"Oh it's no trouble to me. Two lemonades and be quick about it," she said.

"Yes Madam." Brian said and went in the kitchen door.

When he returned Jeff was lying naked on the bed face down and Jill was massaging cream into his lower back and buttocks. He put the drinks on the table.

"About time," Jill said, "now get on with your work."

"Yes Madam."

"But first, you are not suitably dressed for housework on a hot day like this. You would be far cooler in a cotton dress. You will find several in my wardrobe but put a slip on underneath and for goodness sake get a move on, or you won't be finished before it is lunch time."

Brian was so excited he could hardly speak, but he managed a, "Yes Madam" as he turned away.

"Report back here when you have finished those chores." Jill said as he went through the door.

Jeff could not believe what he was hearing, but he said nothing. Brian hurried up the stairs and being very familiar with his wife's wardrobe he quickly found a slip he had always fancied wearing and, as a sort of bonus, he found the matching knickers. He already knew the dress he wanted and within five minutes he was coming downstairs in a short sleeved blue dress trimmed with white piping. He was tying on his apron as he came down the stairs. There was not a lot of clearing up to do, so it was only about twenty minutes when he appeared on the patio.

Jill was still massaging cream into Jeff's body, but now he was face up and it was his penis and genitals that were getting her attention. For the first time Brian noticed that Jeff's erection was probably an inch or so longer than his and noticeably thicker.

"Is there anything else, Madam?" he asked, as Jill looked up from her task.

She looked him up and down with a smile.

"Well yes, girl," she said, "go and get me a packet of condoms and some lubricant."

This time it was less than two minutes before Brian returned with the items. Jill was blatantly masturbating Jeff.

"Get over here, girl, and put a condom on this lovely cock."

Brian could not believe it as he did as ordered. He took one condom out of the packet and slipped the tube of lubricant and the packet into his apron pocket. He had put many condoms on his own penis but his hands were shaking and he was having a lot of trouble. Finally he managed, and Jill who had made her impatience obvious said, "About time too, girl. You will have to have a lot of practise with that. Now get some lube on my pussy and on that cock."

Brian took the tube out of his apron pocket. She was actually going to do it. Jill lay back on her bed and spread her legs. Brian squeezed the tube onto Jeff's rampant cock and spread it down the shaft. Then he went round the bed squeezing more on his fingers and bending down he spread it along the lips of her vulva and gently pushed some inside.

Jill slapped his hand, "get out of the way girl."

Brian stepped back as Jill said, "Get over here big boy," and her hand had grabbed Jeff's arm.

In one movement he rolled onto his feet then knelt between her legs and leant forward.

"Come on you dozy idle cow," Jill said, "guide it in for me and be quick about it."

Almost in a dream Brian found himself on his knees with his fingers round Jeff's cock aiming it at his wife' waiting vagina. That at least he got right, because the next moment Jeff's handsome cock slid into Jill's well lubricated slit and Brian stepped back to view the awesome sight of the mature bronzed man vigorously fucking his wife while he stood petticoated and aproned awaiting orders.

It seemed like an eternity to Brian but it was actually only five minutes before Jill was panting and groaning with a massive orgasm and Jeff pulled his cock out of her. He sat back on the other bed and Jill sat up, "That was lovely Jeff. Thank you."

"It certainly was my dear." Jeff said and looked up at the waiting Brian.

"For goodness sake, girl, get the condom off." Jill snapped and Brian jumped to attend to her order and stood back holding it."

"What is the matter with you, girl?" Jill said, "Are you looking for a thrashing?" Go and get a warm flannel, towel and talc to clean us and get rid of that johnny."

"Yes Madam." Brian said and hurried to the kitchen. He returned very quickly and looked at Jill.

"For goodness sake deal with my guest first, and you should have had those ready before we finished. I don't know what sort of maid are you?"

Brian was wiping and drying the penis that had just cuckolded him when Jeff said, "A maid that is in need of some discipline, I think."

"Quite right, Jeff, and if she is not careful she will get some."

Brian was blushing with embarrassment as he washed and dried his wife's genitals. As he did so Jeff said, "Do you fancy popping down the pub for a drink and spot of lunch my dear?"

"That would be nice I'll just slip into something." She got up and as she went in the house she stopped and looked back at Brian who was still is a state of mild shock. "You girl. Brenda isn't it? Get these beds put away, then wait in the hall for your orders."

Twenty minutes later Jill came down the stairs in a smart summer suit. Brian was standing against the wall, with his hands clasped across his apron.

"Get your hands behind you, girl." Jill snapped and Brian quickly did.

At that moment Jill saw Jeff though the frosted glass panel of the front door. She opened it.

"Come in, Jeff, I am just giving Brenda her orders."

She turned back to her feminised husband and said. "Tidy and dust the dining room and lounge then the hall landing and stairs. If I am not back, stand here with your hands behind your back and wait."

She walked right up to Brian and stared into his eyes, "You do not and I mean do not play with your sissy clit. This afternoon I am going to milk you and I had better get a really good load or you will find a dozen with the riding crop added to the six you are already going to get. Is that clear, girl?"

"Yes Madam," the disappointed Brian said. He had been look forward to relieving himself once Jill had gone out but there was no way he was going to disobey her and break the maid/Mistress relationship they had at this moment.

As Jill turned to leave Jeff said, "Has she got plenty to do this afternoon?"

"No, not a lot."

"I don't suppose I could borrow her to do my bedroom and some ironing for me."

"Of course you could, Jeff. Do you hear that, Brenda; when you have finished here go next door and do what Mr Phillips wants?"

"Thank you," Jeff said, "I have left the door unlocked." He turned to Brian and said, "When you do the bedroom, pick up any clothes and put them in the wash. My shirts are hanging on the kitchen airer. They want ironing and make sure you do them nicely. Oh, you might as well wash up while you are there."

"Yes Sir." Brian said and curtsied to his wife's lover.

Jill and Jeff drove to the pub in silence. They sat down and ordered their food and not until that was done and they had both taken a sip of their drinks, did Jeff say, "Well what was that all about?"

Jill laughed, "Didn't you enjoy it?"

"My God, yes I did. You are so nice and tight but Brian? What was happening?"

"I don't know. Oh, I know he likes to try my undies on and a couple of times I put him in my frilly shortie nightdress then tied him to the bed for a couple of hours while I watch television but that was not very successful."

"Oh why not?"

"Oh well, when I do come up he is lying there with an erection like a telegraph pole, but when I lower myself on he only lasts about three seconds and if I put a condom on him he comes before I have rolled it right down."

"I'm not surprised my dear, but you can get something to put round the base of his prick to stop him coming you know."

"Really that might be worth trying but this housework and maid business is a surprise to me. When we saw you in the garden his reaction told me he wanted me to fuck you, but I was making the bed so I just thought, 'if he wants that, he can do this' and put the apron on him. The rest followed from there.

There was a moment's silence as the waitress put their meals on the table then Jeff said, "I don't think it matters why. What I think is important is how are we going to exploit the situation?"

"What do you mean?"

"Oh, come on Jill. Here you have a man who, as long as he is humiliated properly, can be used as a servant for all sorts of occasions or purposes. He can be used for sex, maybe commercial sex and has not going to object if you fancy a bit on the side. Surely we can dream up some good ideas on how to use him to our advantage.

"I suppose so, have you any suggestions?"

"Well yes I have." And Jeff started to explain his ideas to Jill.

When he had finished Jill said "Just a minute, Jeff, he is my husband. I'm not sure its fair to do that."

"My dear he has shown you how he wants to be treated, but take my word for it he will feel guilty about it from time to time and get upset. My idea will get rid of his guilt and give you stability in your relationship."

"Okay, we'll give it a try."

When they got back Brian was just finishing ironing Jeff's shirts.

"What's this?" Jill demanded, "You should have finished this, girl. You've been idling. That will be six with the riding crop."

"Please Madam, I haven't."

"Arguing with me, eh!" Right that's an extra three."

She could see that Brian was getting excited again at the treatment so maybe Jeff was right.

"Finish that and get back to my house quick."

"Yes Madam."

When Brian got back Jill was sitting having a drink in the lounge.

"Right girl. Mr Phillips is coming to dinner. I have written out what we are going to have so you get into that kitchen and start preparing the vegetables. When you have done that get changed into the clothes I have laid on the bed for you and then lay the table for two. You will serve dinner."

"Yes Madam," the now very excited Brian said.

As soon as he was in the kitchen Jill picked up the phone and rang Jeff, "He's busy; have you got the stuff. Yes. Good. Bring it over."

It was a very pleasant dinner. Jeff and Jill sat chatting and enjoying each other's company while Jill's new maid, looking very smart in the black dress and white apron Jill had found for her, served, poured wine or stood by the wall with her hands clasped in front of his apron. She was well behaved, except for one occasion when Jill had to speak sharply to her for fidgeting. Brian realised that she would notice, because she had arranged the table so Jeff and her sat at one corner of the table with their backs to the bookcase while he stood in front of them beside the sideboard.

When they finished their sweet Jill said, "You may clear Brenda. My guest and I are going into the lounge. Serve coffee in there in fifteen minutes."

Brian started to pick up the plates as the couple stood up. They watched him leave with the dirty crockery and Jeff went to the bookcase and removed a book. Then they went into the lounge.

By the time Brian served coffee the Jill and her lover were sitting on the couch. Brian noticed they had moved it slightly so it no longer faced directly at the television. He assumed that this was to give them a better view of how he came into the room carrying the coffee tray.

"That will do, Brenda." Jill said, "Go and finish the washing up then report back here."

Brian was now getting into the spirit of the scene and with a neat curtsey he said, "Yes Madam"

As he left the room Jill said "Oh and bring the condoms and some lubricant with you."

"Yes Madam."

By the time Brian returned Jill and Jeff were doing some deep kissing and fondling.

"Oh Brenda come here." Jill ordered and when he was standing in front of them she said, "You may get us ready, girl. Suck my guest and lubricate me."

Brian was so excited. This was so humiliating, he thought he would faint, but he knelt down in front of the lovers and did as ordered. In seconds Jeff's erection was like iron and Jill's vagina was slippery with natural and artificial lubricant.

Brian pulled away from Jeff's penis but gently stroked it with his hand, "I think you guest is ready Madam." He said.

"Right then, girl, get the condom on him." Jill snapped and Brian quickly obeyed. He suddenly had to shuffle quickly back as Jill swung herself over Jeff's legs and impaled herself on his rampant and well-prepared erection.

Brian watched as Jill, with her head buried in Jeff's shoulder and neck, worked herself up and down until with a grunt from Jeff and a cry from Jill they both climaxed.

After the maid had tidied the lovers up she was sent to wait in the kitchen and was still there when Jill said goodnight to their neighbour.

"Right girl." Jill said when she went in there. " Finish clearing up. I am going to have a bath and get to bed. You can use the shower. Put that pretty blue nightie of mine on and get into bed as quick as you can."

For the third time that day Jill had excellent sex. It was true Brian was not quite and big or experienced as Jeff but he was very excited and did his best to please her.

The next morning it was as if none of it had happened. At work Brian was wondering if it had all been a dream, at the same time feeling somewhat guilty for allowing himself to he humiliated in that fashion. Brian did not mention the incident the next day nor did Jill at least to Brian. She took an hour of work on the Wednesday and went to Jeff's office. Here she viewed the edited version of the secret video that Jeff had taken. At no time were their faces shown but Brian was easily recognisable as the feminised obedient maid.

The lovers discussed their further actions.

"But Jeff he is my husband," Jill said, "I am not sure I can do this to him."

"My dear we discussed this. It is for his own good. I can assure you he will feel guilty about allowing all that to happen. However he won't be able to resist doing it again. This way there will be no guilt because you will be forcing him to do it. Also being made to do it will increase his excitement and at the end of the day you will get an obedient and efficient house-maid."

"And you will get a convenient and cheap whore to use."

Jeff grinned, " And a part time maid I hope."

"Oh I suppose so, but he can't go on wearing my dresses."

"Of course not. Let us make a list of what he will need, then I will order the uniforms through our overall supplier, they will deliver tomorrow and you can buy his undies at lunchtime tomorrow.

"And you still think I should make him sleep in the box room."

"Of course. I don't want my Mistress sleeping with the servant, but you can always order her into your room if you feel the need for her services."

By Friday evening Brian was wondering if there was to be a repeat of last weekend. When he got home Friday Jill was already there.

"Go and sit in the lounge darling," she said, "I'll bring you a drink. I have a video I would like to see."

Brian sat opposite the television as Jill started the tape.

His eyes came out like organ stops as he watched and his penis started to twitch and stiffen uncontrollably. It was immediately obvious to him that he was clearly recognisable, whilst neither Jill nor Jeff were. When it had finished Jill said, "What do you think of that dear? Oh Jeff and I have our own copies by the way, so that one is yours to keep."

"What are you going to do with it?"

"Well my darling. We could show it to your workmates or friends. I'm sure they would love to see it."

"You wouldn't."

"Not unless I had a good reason to do so."

"What do you want?"

Jill visibly relaxed and sprawled back in the chair, "Why my dear, a hard working, faithful and obedient house/parlour maid."

"You mean you want to do the same thing this weekend as last Sunday?"

Jill laughed "No, no. If you go up to your room, which is what we used to call the box room, you will find your uniforms in the wardrobe. In the drawers there are your undies and on the dressing table your make-up. Also on the dressing table is your work schedule. You will see that you are to be my maid every evening and all weekends. That is except for the times you are working for Mr Phillips."

Brian's erection was so big that Jill could clearly see the bulge in his trousers, so she knew she was on the right lines. So she went on, "Oh and Brenda, Mr Philips says that it would not be right for me, the Mistress of the house, to sleep with the servant. So you will sleep in the box room."

"No, please Madam." Brian said not very conscious of his need to have sexual relief right away.

"Oh yes my girl. I think Mr Phillips will be able to keep me content in that department and if I do fancy using you then I just have to call you to the room."

She laughed again when she saw the look on her husband's face. She was enjoying this more than the thought she would.

"Now Brenda we do realise that this may be a little frustrating for you so later this evening Mr Phillips is bringing round a device which, he assures me, will prevent you having an erection once it is locked in position. So that will take care of that."

Jill stood up and looked down at her crestfallen husband.

"Now get up to your room and get changed. I have put your black and white uniform on the bed for this evening, as you will serve dinner. One place only. Mr Phillips will be round later to fit your chastity device himself. I am really looking forward to that."

With that Brian got up and after looking closely at his wife to make sure she was serious he said, "Very good Madam. I will try and make you a good maid. May I go now?"

"Oh yes Brenda carry on." And she felt a shiver of excitement up she spine as she watched her now subservient husband leave the room knowing he was fully under her control

A Job Opportunity

Peter was not too concerned when the collapse came. He had only been with the firm for just over a year but he got quite a generous pay off. He was only in a tiny bed-sit and had an old banger of a car. If he had to move to get a new job he could with little trouble. He registered with a local job agency that would find him some temporary work while he was looking.

"It is quite a big room," Mrs Morris said, "My husband's aunt had it converted from the old stables. She was an artist and sculptress hence it's a workshop come lounge."

"I see." Peter said noting the door into the main house and another to an enclosed flight of stairs to what must be a large loft. "What did you want me to do Mrs Morris?"

"Ah yes well you see that great heap of clothes and ornaments."

"Yes."

"I want you to go though them. The ornaments need carefully packing and lis☐ing in those boxes and then will be going to an auction house. You have a good look at the clothes. Any too old and tatty put in a sack, the others divide up. You know, coats, skirts, dresses etc. Fold and pack them in the boxes. I will be sending them to my charity. Can you manage that?"

Could he manage that? All those ladies clothes, couldn't he just!

"I think so, Mrs Morris."

Peter started sorting and packing, but all the time he was eyeing those clothes. From what he could see they were rather old fashioned, fifties, sixties maybe even twenties and thirties. He would get a closer look, but would he get a chance to try any of the on? Mrs Morris kept popping out of the kitchen door to see how he was getting on.

Eventually she called him in to have some lunch and as he went in the door he spotted, on the back of the pile, a rubber raincoat. It was dark blue and he could see no sleeves. Was it a cape? Women's capes had fascinated him as long as he could remember. He just had to see.

He finished the packing by five o'clock. Mr Morris had come home. It appeared he was a self-employed plumber.

"Keep at it lad," he said, "I need to move my equipment in here next week"

"Yes, Mr Morris."

As Peter got into his car Mrs Morris said, "be here early in the morning. I have to go to London and need to give you some instructions."

Peter's heart gave a bound. Mrs Morris in London, Mr Morris at work and all those lovely clothes.

He arrived early as instructed.

"Now," Mrs Morris said, "I have left you some sandwiches and a flask of coffee. I will be gone until quite late and Mr Morris has a big central heating job to do so he won't be back until the evening. Pack anything decent in the boxes. Put any worn out stuff in the bags and put them in your car. In the morning take them to the council tip, then come and see me and I will pay you plus any expenses. Do you understand?"

"Oh yes Mrs Morris, but what if I have finished before you come back?"

"Just slam the door before you go."

At that moment Mr Morris put his head round the door.

"Come on darling I'll drop you off at the station."

"Okay." His wife replied and she gave Peter a big smile, a pat on the cheek and said, "See you then. Have a good time and take anything you fancy." With that she stepped through the kitchen door laughing at her own joke.

Peter could not believe it. First he walked from the back yard, where his car was parked round the front of the house to make sure they actually gone. Then he came back. He grabbed the raincoat. Yes it was a cape. Just the sort he liked, with armholes and a hood that would drape over his head. He was tempted to put it on but no. First he would get dressed. He had all day. He would wear a dress at least until two or three o'clock. He could do his job as a girl. It was nearly too much for him.

There were all sorts of undies, but best was a corselet and he could not believe his luck as he pulled it on. It fitted. A bit tight, but that was all to the good. He found a pile of stockings and enjoyed checking them for ladders and selected a matching pair, then slipping them on and for the first time fastening six suspenders. He was wearing plain black slip-on shoes, which were not quite right, but they did not look too much out of place. Next it was knickers. He eventually picked out a nice pair of pale blue French knickers with nice frills and embroidery, which had a matching petticoat. Then he decided on a dark green linen dress, which buttoned up the front with pretty white buttons, which came down almost to his ankles. As he picked up the dress a pale green mop cap with a white trim fell on the floor. He could recall seeing something similar on sale in a department store with, what they called, a hostess apron. He delved through the pile and found the matching bibbed apron. Perfect! Just right for working in. He was just about to slip the apron on and get to work when he thought, no, a little treat first and he picked up the cape and put it round his shoulders.

Ten minutes swishing up and down in the lovely cape and then Peter, now capped and aproned, settled down to his task.

He had had his lunch and was just getting started again when the kitchen door opened. Peter froze.

"Well, well," Mr Morris said, "what do we have here?"

Peter was paralysed as Mr Morris walked over to him, looking him up and down.

"Very nice," he said, "that suits you and they fit nicely."

Mr Morris clearly was not angry so Peter said, "I'm sorry Mr Morris. I thought you were working all day. Mrs Morris said I could have anything I wanted."

Mr Morris nodded, "Oh the suppliers sent the wrong fittings so I can't finish till tomorrow and of course you can have what you want." He looked round and spotted Peter's clothes on a bench against the wall. He picked them up.

"You don't want to get these mixed up and pack them by mistake," he said "I'll look after them for you." And he walked back through the kitchen door. As he did so he said over his shoulder.

"Carry on girl. I'll call you if I need you."

Peter stood still recovering from the shock. He was stuck. Mr Morris had his clothes and his car keys. What could he do? Just carry on he thought. So he did.

About half an hour later Mr Morris came back. He had clearly just showered and was wearing a pair of lightweight trousers and a polo shirt.

"I will be in the lounge watching a video," he said, "there is some cold beef in the fridge. Make me a couple of sandwiches and server them in the lounge."

Peter looked at him with a puzzled look on his face.

"You can make sandwiches I suppose?"

"Yes, Mr Morris."

"Good. Then get on with it, put some pickle on them. Oh and you can call me Sir now on."

"Err yes, Sir."

Mr Morris walked back thought the door and Peter followed.

By time he had found everything and had made the sandwiches 20 minutes had passed. He knocked on the lounge door and, at the command to 'enter', went in.

Mr Morris was sitting in the armchair drinking a beer from the bottle.

"Put them there, girl." He said pointing to a coffee table.

As Peter went to do so he could see the screen. It was a scene in and office setting and a man in a smart business suit was sitting in an executive chair with his legs sprawled, his flies open and his semi-erect penis sticking out. Between them knelt a girl dressed in a smart grey costume like a secretary would wear.

"Come Miss Jones," the man was saying, "just get on with your job."

As he said this his hand went to the back of the girl's head and pulled it down until her lips went round he head of his rapidly stiffening cock and she started to suck.

Peter had put the food down and was watching the television.

"That will be all, girl." Mr Morris said, "Get back in the kitchen and make me a pot of coffee. Serve it on a tray in fifteen minutes."

"Yes sir." Peter said and his penis was stiffening rapidly from the combination of the scene on the television and being treated like a serving girl.

As he went out of the door Mr Morris said, "Did I see some nylons on the table?"

"Yes Sir."

"Bring me a pair when you come back."

"Yes Sir."

Fifteen minutes later Peter was again knocking on the door. As he entered Mr Morris picked up the remote and froze the tape.

As he stood up he said, "Put the coffee down there." pointing to the coffee table.

Peter did so then stood up. The stockings were draped over his arm and he took them and offered them to Mr Morris.

"Mr Morris took them with a smile and said, "Turn round girl," Peter did so, "hands behind you," was the next order and as Peter obeyed he felt two strong hands take his wrists. The next moment his hands were firmly bound behind him.

"Right girl, go and stand in that corner until I want you." Mr Morris said, pointing to a corner behind him.

"Yes sir." Peter said "But please Sir, why have you tied me up?"

Mr Morris chuckled, "To keep you out of mischief. I know what naughty things you sissy boys can get up to."

As Peter went to his corner Mr Morris sat down and started the tape again.

Peter looked at it. The characters were still there but the scene had changed. It was a very ornate room and through an open door he could see two coloured men sitting in armchairs. To one side and in the forefront was middle-aged coloured woman wearing an elaborate dress and lots of jewellery. Facing her were the two characters Peter had seen before.

"Now my dear, the man was saying. You know this it for the best. You know we have a desperate cash flow problem."

"Yes sir," the young lady replied, "but does it have to be here?"

"Well my dear, Madam Ebony here is a good friend of mine and she will look after you. Also she has mainly black clients and they will pay well for a nice fresh white girl and the company gets 50% of everything you earn. You must do your best to please the clients because the company will also get all of any tips they give you."

"But what do I get?"

With this the coloured woman grabbed the girl's arm. "You get room and board and a thrashing if you don't do as you're told. Now come on and lets get you into your working clothes."

As she pulled the girl away the man said, "Don't worry about your flat my dear. My new secretary will take it over, as you want be need it any more."

With that the man walked out chuckling and the scene closed.

Peter looked back at Mr Morris. He was doing something with in his crotch. "Get over here, girl." He said.

Peter walked slowly round the chair. As he did so he saw that Mr Morris had his penis out and was gently playing with it.

"On your knees, girl. Right here." He said pointing to the space between his spread legs.

Peter walked round until he was right in front of Mr Morris.

Something was compelling him to so as he was told but he said, "No, please Sir."

"Get on your knees right now and lets have no more nonsense from you."

Peter dropped to his knees and his face was just a little higher that the rigid penis Mr Morris was now sporting. Mr Morris put his hand behind Peter's head just like the man did in the video and also just like that man he said, Come Miss Jones. Just get on with your job." And he chuckled.

As Peter's lips circled the bulbous head of the cock he felt a surge of excitement. He was dressed as a girl, had been treated like a maidservant and was now being treated just like the girl in the video. For one wild moment he wondered if Mr Morris was going to sell him to a brothel as that girl had been sold, and his penis oozed pre-cum into his knickers. He sucked and licked for less than two minutes before, what seemed like, gallons of semen gushed into the back of his throat. He swallowed hard.

Mr Morris patted his head, "Good girl," he said, "up you get."

When they were both standing. Mr Morris said, "Come on I have to go out." He walked quickly to the studio and Peter followed.

As Mr Morris walked across to the door that led to the loft he took a couple of spanners from the toolbox on the bench. Unlocking the door he lead Peter up the stairs to a large loft with boxes and bits of equipment lying about.

"Turn round." Mr Morris ordered and when Peter did so he untied his hands. "Now help me with this," and he went to a pile of metal frames with bars in them. While Peter held and gripped as ordered Mr Morris fitted bars, nuts and screws plus a wooden platform all together until, with a heave, he had a cage with a door and wooden base on the floor.

"Get in." Mr Morris ordered, and after a moment's hesitation Peter crept in. The cage was tall but not tall enough to stand up in, except in the middle where the bars forming the top had a round hole welded in place.

"Stand up and put your head out." Was the next order, and as Peter did so Mr Morris reached over and fastened a collar round his neck. There was a click and it was locked in position with a padlock. Peter realised that there was no way he could lower himself again as the collar had spikes sticking out of it which were too big to go down the hole. Mr Morris shut the cage door and put another padlock on it. He looked at his handiwork and said, "Very good, that will work well." He laughed

"Now since you've been a good girl we'll have the collar off, but bear in mind what can happen if you misbehave."

He produced some keys and removed the collar. Peter crouched down and then sat in the corner of the cage.

"I am going to collect the fittings for tomorrow," Mr Morris said, "then I will collect Mrs Morris from the station. You can wait there. I can't wait to see the look on her face when she sees you dressed like that."

With that he went down the stairs and Peter heard the door slam at the bottom.

All Peter could do was to sit and wait in his cage. He calculated that over three hours had passed and it was dark when he heard the door open and footsteps coming up the stairs. The light came on and Mrs and Mr Moore walked into the room and over to the cage.

Mrs Moore stood looking at him and grinning. "Well you're right Jack, this is a surprise but maybe a nice one. Get her out."

Mr Moore unlocked the door, "Out, you," he ordered and Peter crept out and stood in front of his employers.

"Over in the light where I can get a good look at you," Mrs Moore said and when Peter did as ordered she slowly walked round him pulling his dress straight and flicking his apron.

"I suppose you have used the little tart already," she said to her husband

"Well darling, you know me. Always ready."

"And how was she?"

"Well it was only a blow job, but she did well and was very obedient."

"Hum!" Mrs Morris said, "You know what we were discussing at the weekend?"

"About the domestic arrangements?"

"Yes."

"Well what about them?"

"Duh! What about this girl? Would she do?"

"I don't see why not. Maybe need some training, but that would apply to anyone you took on and with her I don't think it will be difficult."

"I think you're right and she will be cheaper to use."

"Well let's give it a go then."

"Okay." Mrs Moore said and she walked round Peter again and stopped in front of him.

"Listen sissy boy," she said, "we are both working and this is a big house. We need a hardworking obedient maid to look after the place and us. Are you interested in the job?"

Peter could not believe his ears. A job as a maid and presumably wearing girl's clothes "Oh yes please, Madam." he replied.

"I can't interview you here; I'll give you fifteen minutes to get yourself tidied up then report to the lounge for a proper interview."

"Yes, Madam."

Peter could hardly wait; the fifteen minutes seemed like an hour before he felt it was time to tap on the door.

"Come in." was the order and he walked in. Mr and Mrs Morris were seated on the settee and he walked over to them and curtsied.

"Now girl," Mrs Morris said, "let's make the situation crystal clear. You are applying for a job as our live in maid is that correct?"

"Yes, Madam."

"What experience have you had?"

"Please Madam, I have had to do all my own cooking, laundry and cleaning for the past four years and I am very willing to learn."

"I see. What is your situation at the moment? Accommodation, family, assets etc.?"

"I live in a bedsit with a week's notice. I have a car and some small savings. I have no close relatives in the country."

"I see in that case we will give you a try. You will work for your keep. We may give you a small allowance when and if you prove to be satisfactory. You will be kept and treated as a girl. You will get no time off. Punishments will be given when necessary, with the strap."

She paused then went on, "Oh and we are planning to hold some interesting parties in the loft once all the equipment is set up. You will have a very active part in those. We are also concerned that being dressed as a girl will cause you to have some sexual arousal and any attempts at masturbation would be a waste of our time and your energy. So we intend to fit you with a chastity device and you will have to earn any relief that we may grant you. Is that all clear?"

"Yes Madam."

"And you are still willing to accept the position bearing in mind that we will take control of all your assets, so while we will be able to dismiss you, you will not be able to leave."

Peter could resist them no longer. As he said, "Oh yes please, Madam." He fell on his knees and started to kiss her dusty boots.

Mrs Morris looked at her husband with raised eyebrows and then, smiling down at the mop cap now bobbing up and down as Peter cleaned her footwear she said, "All right girl. You're ours from now on and your name will be." She stopped for a moment, "Yes, Alice, I think. That is a good name for a maid. Stop that now girl, we have to get dinner ready."

"Yes Madam." Peter said and stood up. He watched as his new Mistress stood up then said. "Please Madam, can I ask a question?"

Mrs Morris looked him up and down. "I suppose so but don't make a habit of it."

"Please Madam, will I have proper maid's uniforms?"

Mrs Morris laughed, "Of course you will, you stupid girl. I am hoping you have enough money to pay for your own to start but we will want everyone who sees you to know immediately your position and status in the household. Now, is there anything else before I put you to work?"

"Yes, please Madam. There is a rubber rain cape with those clothes. May I have that to go shopping in?"

Mrs Morris laughed even louder. "You silly girl, of course you can, in fact your can have any of those clothes you like; particularly the undies, as all your clothes will be disposed of. Now come on and stop your nonsense or you will get the strap."

Mrs Morris turned and strode of to the kitchen. With a contented sigh Peter followed her to start his new life.

Loo Lady

Ann Wilkinson could hardly stop herself laughing and she could not stop a faint smile as she looked at Tim Harvey standing in front of her desk, looking so woebegone in his green dress and tabard.

It was nearly twenty years since Tim Black, Julie Winters and her had been at school together. At one time she had quite fancied Tim but one day, during their last month at school, she and Julie had been clearing out a storeroom. It was the sight of Julie in tight fitting nylon overall that made her realise that it was Julie she was more interested in. She grabbed her and kissed her. It was a pleasant surprise when Julie responded and a few minutes later she had the girl on her knees licking her fanny.

It came as a bit of the blow when Tim and Julie decided to get married.

To show no hard feelings, Ann was Julie's bridesmaid and after they came back from honeymoon all three of the school pals began working at Wilkinson's.

Ann was George Wilkinson's secretary when his wife died. She did her best to help and support him during the arrangements for the funeral and for the actual day she bought a black rubberised satin cape and hood. It was this garment that got her where she was today.

Ann had organised the refreshments at the house and eventually she saw all the guests and the caterers out, leaving just her and her boss. She put her cape on ready to go and George thanked her. He put his arms round her and hugged her close. With her arms trapped in her cape she could not resist but she felt the hardness of his erection pressing into her thigh.

"Oh my God, Ann," he said in a quivery voice, "I don't want to be left on my own." and he kissed her full on the lips.

He didn't turn Ann on, but his money did. Before too many minutes had passed George was naked and spread-eagled on her cape, which was now over his double bed, and she was sucking his surprisingly large cock.

Six weeks later they were married and Ann was made joint managing director. Tim was company cashier and Ann got Julie promoted to personnel manager.

George could not have been happier. Ann found a girl called Betty who was a divorcee in her mid thirties and an excellent cook/housekeeper.

If George had his way he would have made love to his young wife every night and all the weekend, but Ann insisted that this would be too much for him. They had separate bedrooms and about three nights a week Ann would get into her nightie, then throwing her cape over it and with the hood draped over her head she made her way to George's room where he waited with a massive hard on. Ann would make it last half and hour or so until she finished him off in various ways. George would turn over and go contentedly to sleep and Ann with her cape round her shoulders would make her way back to her room confident that her slave would be kneeling by the bed, eyes down and waiting to satisfy her Mistress. Betty did not see her Mistress enter but she heard the rustle of her cape as she strode over to the dressing table to pick up the riding crop, so she could teach her slave her true place in the household.

It was probably too much sex, which killed George, but at least he died happy.

It was when Ann took over all the reins of the business that she found Tim's deception. He had been milking the funds for years. Ann had all the proof she needed. When she and Julie faced him, he could not deny it.

"I don't know what he has been spending it on." Julie said.

They soon found out. He had a little flat in town and wardrobes full of tarty clothes, all in Tim's size. At first they thought it was to keep a Mistress in but Tim soon convinced them that he used it to dress up as a lady or a maid or sometimes a tart.

Julie was disgusted but she did not want her husband in prison.

"Can't we find some other way?" she pleaded.

"Well, he will have to sign a full confession." Ann said.

"I will, I will." Tim was eager to co-operate

"And we will pay the money back somehow." Julie said.

"Now let's not be hasty. It is quite lot and I don't think you should suffer for what this stupid man has done. I'll tell you what, if Tim signs the confession and then agrees to whatever punishment we decide, I will arrange to buy the flat as a company asset and with the money Tim can repay the debt."

"Yes, yes," Tim said, "I will do anything you say."

Ann pushed over a pad and pen.

"Put it all down. Everything you know, dates, time amounts. You stay in this office until it is done."

Tim started to write and Ann took Julie by the arm.

"Coming for some coffee."

"I am very sorry about this Ann," Julie said.

"Don't worry about it. Now you are quite sure you want me to punish him?"

"Oh yes, but what will you do with him?"

"Just you wait my girl. I will make the punishment fit the crime or at least part of it."

Ann took her hand and squeezed it.

"How about coming round for dinner one evening next week. We could have a nice cosy evening you and I."

"I'd like to Ann, but haven't you got your housekeeper. Betty isn't it?"

Ann laughed. "Don't worry about Betty. It will do the little slut good to know that she is not going to get my full attention in the future. Since George died she thinks she's got exclusive rights to my body and my riding crop. And you, my little chicken, need a few red stripes across your arse."

Julie grinned, "Yes Mistress. Just to keep me in my place?"

"Too right. I'll have the pair of you naked bent over side by side. "

When they got back to the office Tim was just sitting.

"Have you finished?" Ann demanded

"Yes Ann."

"Then!" she yelled "Why are you not standing in the corner facing the wall, and it's Madam to you from now on."

Half an hour later, with the help of a couple of girls from the office, the document was signed, dated and witnessed.

When the girls had gone she said, "Tim I am going to appoint your assistant, Jason, to your post. You have a month to put the accounts straight."

"What shall I do after that Madam?"

"I don't know yet, but I am thinking about it. You may go both of you. Don't forget my place for dinner Tuesday, Julie."

They were going out of the door when Julie turned and said, "Oh I nearly forgot I needed to see you about another matter."

Ann waved her back in

"Well what is it?"

I have had a complaint from the cleaning supervisor. You know the cleaners are all women. They clean the men's toilets every day. They put a notice outside the door and it takes about half and hour. Now the lads can go to one of the toilets on the other floors but they can't be bothered so they push the notice away and walk in.

"I see, a bit embarrassing then."

"Not just that, several of the cleaners have complained about sexual harassment."

"I see. Okay I'll do something about it."

"You could try talking to the lads on the shop floor."

"I could and I will, but I think I have an idea that may solve the problem."

Ann did have a word and the situation improved for a couple of weeks, but it soon deteriorated.

At the end of the four weeks Tim reported that he had cleared everything and that his assistant had taken over.

"What do I do now Madam?"

Julie was sitting by her boss and the two ladies looked at the man standing in front of them.

"I have another job for you Tim," Ann said slowly, "you will be solving a problem and providing a very important service."

"What is it Madam?"

"You are going to be the permanent cleaner of the men's toilets in the factory."

Julie gave a shriek of laughter, "you sneaky cow," she said, and laughed some more.

"I can't do that." Tim objected

"You can and you will."

"This is the punishment you thought up, is it?"

"Oh no, Tim this is a job for which you will get paid at your old salary. I don't want Julie to suffer so your cheque will be handed over to her every month. She can give you any allowance she thinks fit."

Tim looked at his wife, "So this is the punishment you two have dreamed up. Keeping me under your control."

Julie's eyes opened wide "This is the first I have heard of it."

"She's right Tim, but this is not your punishment either."

"Well, what is it then?"

"You are going to work under the cleaning supervisor Mrs Stevens, and you will wear the same uniform as the other cleaning staff."

"But we haven't got any male cleaners."

"Exactly."

Tim went white, "No please, you can't."

"Oh yes I can, Tina. I have talked to Mrs Stevens and she is quite looking forward to training you. All her staff think it's a good idea, so that is what will happen. You start Monday." That gives you this week to get your uniforms and to get some practise at wearing them at home."

"Not that you need practise in wearing female clothes but you need some at obeying orders. I'm sure Julie will help you with that."

"Won't I just!" Julie said with obvious enthusiasm.

"No, no, please, I can't."

"Must I remind you that you agreed to accept my punishment, and this is it. You know the alternative and I am sure that if you went to prison we could find a way of letting the other inmates know about your odd habits."

"You would too, you bitch. I suppose I've got no choice."

"No and the name is Madam not bitch. I think you need a little reminder of your new position in life. Will you attend to that for me Julie when you get Tina home."

"Certainly, Ann." Julie said getting to her feet "Come on Tina. We will get you some undies and uniforms on Monday but for now I will find you some old stuff of mine."

Ann smiled as she watched the beaten man follow his wife out of the room.

Tim did not know how he was going to face it. A week obeying his wife, and working for her as a housemaid had helped. She had made it quite clear that, even when he was working he would still be expected to do her housework in the evenings and weekends.

The cleaners started at 7 am but Julie was very kind the first day and took him, dressed in his smart new uniform, in the car.

"As from tomorrow it's the bus for you my girl," she told him, "but I have got a present for you from Ann."

She reached into the hall cupboard and pulled out the black rain cape that had served Ann so well.

"This will keep you dry in the rain," she said, "come on, slip this on."

"Ah Tina." Mrs Stevens said as Tim came into the cleaner's staff room. There had been no absentees in the cleaning staff that morning and all the girls were gathered round.

"This is Tina, girls," She said, "it used to be Mr Harvey and he used to have some authority, but no longer. You will treat her like any other girl, except she is on permanent gents toilet-cleaning and is the lowest ranking member of staff. Now I know that any new starter is automatically the lowest rank but in Tina's case we have special instructions. She always will be the lowest even if new staff arrive."

" Oh yes, Mrs Stevens." They all chorused.

"The least ranking member of staff makes and serves the tea Tina, and that is you from now on. I will show you the job for the next couple of days. Then you are on your own. That's your trolley over there. Get it and follow me."

Tim had to walk through the ranks of cleaners to his trolley. Mrs Stevens had turned and opened the door and she did not see hands going up his skirts, pinching his legs, tugging his knickers or snapping his suspenders but she heard the comments.

"Now that is enough ladies," she said, "there is work to be done. Tea break is the time to relax."

With a general laugh the girls parted and let the blushing feminised Tim push his trolley to the door.

For the first three days is was not so bad. Mrs Stevens put the notices outside the loo doors and while she was there nobody came in. Of course Tim had to put up with teasing when he served the tea to the other cleaners.

Mrs Stevens used the management canteen so there was nobody to restrain the ladies. However the novelty soon wore off and by the third day they were treating Tim as a sort of maidservant

On the fourth morning Mrs Stevens escorted Tim to the first loo.

"Now you are on your own Tina. I will be inspecting your work. I understand we can't sack you or dock your wages so I will have to think up some other form of discipline for you, but don't worry I'll think of something."

She took the notice that they stood outside the door and showed it to Tim.

"It no longer matters if the men come in while you are working so we have had your notice specially made."

Tim looked at it. It was the standard notice say, "CLEANING IN PROGRESS", but instead of going on, "NO ENTRY", it now said, "ENTER AT YOUR OWN RISK".

With little chuckle Mrs Stevens walked to the door.

"Don't worry, I'll put it outside for you"

It was not long. The news had already gone round the factory that they were having a male cleaner wearing the same uniform as the girls and whom it was. The foreman, Joe Green and two of his charge hands took early tea and arrived just as Tim was cleaning the first toilet bowl.

"Well, well look what we have here lads. A nice little nancy boy."

Tim stood up, turned and started to come out.

"Oh no Nancy boy," Joe said, "you are in the right place. We will be gentle with you at first. Sit down!" He pushed Tim backwards so he sat on the loo seat.

"Me first lads," Joe said and unzipped his flies. A large semi erect cock flopped out.

"Now nancy," the man said, "you can have it easy or hard. Either you do just as you're told or we strip you down to your undies and tie you over the loo with you legs well spread. What's it going to be?"

Tim realised he had no choice. He had, at times, dressed himself up as a tart and imagined being a prostitute, but now it was for real and he was not sure.

"Well!" the man demanded

"All right." He said in a quavery voice, "What do you want with me?"

"A nice blow job you stupid bitch. Now get this in your gob and get on with it. We only get 15 minutes tea break and there are three of us."

Tim found a now hard cock pushed between his lips and the started to suck. It was only a few moments in fact and the man's semen was pumping out into his throat."

"Swallow it slut," the man growled and Tim did.

The man withdrew and the next one stood there with his cock hard as rock. Tim quickly gave a repeat performance and once again was rewarded with a mouthful of semen. He looked for the next customer, but to his surprise the next man's cock was hanging limp. The man however held it between his fingers.

"Sorry nancy," he said, "I gave the missus a good seeing to this morning. I only came in for a slash. Open wide."

More in surprise that anything else Tim did as he was ordered and a stream of warm piss hit the back of this throat. With a gulp he managed to start swallowing. The man however was considerate and he controlled the flow with his fingers so that Tim had time to swallow it all.

The charge hand was laughing as he fastened his zip.

"All right nancy," Joe said, "you've done well for a start. You are my tart now. Nobody will bother you without asking me first. Tomorrow we will start teaching you to take it up your arse. Now get back to your scrubbing."

Joe was as good as his word and nobody troubled him as he worked his way round the toilets. Eventually he came to the office toilets and as he was cleaning the second cubicle Jason Briggs came in.

He looked at his old boss with a broad grin.

"Tina isn't it?" he said

"Yes Sir."

"I must say the boss has got you where she wants you and Joe Green has as well."

"Yes Sir."

"You know what he is going to do with you, don't you?"

"Not really Sir."

"As I understand it he is going to rent you out as a sort of male prostitute."

"What! Are you sure?"

"Yes he has asked me to get come chits made. A, B, and H on different chits with a place for a fee, date, time and a signature."

"What for?"

Jason was enjoying himself and he grinned even more as he said, "It means Arse. Blow Job or Hand. So I am told. If one of the lads fancies using you he will see Joe. Joe will charge him a fee for whatever service he wants, then sign and give him the correct chit. He brings it to you and you provide the service and keep the chit."

Tim went white, "But he will be pimping me."

Jason shrugged, "Oh yes but it's all above board. You keep the chits and hand them to me. I collect the cash from Joe. He gets a 20% cut shared with his two mates and the rest goes in the staff welfare fund. It will be quite useful. It will go towards the staff Christmas party."

Jason laughed again as he watched Tim's face.

"Quite funny, really," He said "as I understand it not only will you be financing the party but you will be working as a maid to get it ready and clear up after. You are going to be quite useful and a good laugh."

With that Jason went back to work chuckling.

Tim thought about what Jason had said for the rest of the day. He had to do something about it and as it neared time to go home he was knocking on Ann's door.

"Well what is it Tina?" she said.

"Please Madam. I have just found out that Joe Green intends to use me as a prostitute."

"What!" the two ladies said together.

"Tell me." Ann ordered and Tim told her the full story which had both of them smiling before he finished.

"I'll soon check on this." Ann said and picked up her internal phone and was soon speaking to her foreman.

She listened for a few minutes the she said, "No I am sorry Joe but she is not company property you know. She belongs to Julie."

She listened again then said, "No Joe, Julie gets 5%, it does not affect Tina's work, and you sort the rest out with Jason as you wish."

She put the phone down and looked at Julie, "That's fixed. You get 5% of whatever they make. Jason will make sure it is all above board. Of course you do what you want with any tips she gets."

"Okay by me Ann." Julie said.

Ann turned to her new toilet cleaner.

"That is all settled, Tina. Now go and get your cape. Your Mistress will be going home shortly.

Tim was appalled. She was not going to do anything about it.

"Please, Madam," he said, "I thought you might help me."

Ann looked at him and nodded, "So I will, Tina."

She pulled open a desk draw took out some items which she pushed over the desk.

"Here you are my dear these should help."

Tim looked at them. One was a large packet of condoms and beside it a big tube of lubricating gel.

Ann smiled at the horrified look on his face. "Now my dear makes sure that if they want to fuck you they wear a condom and you put plenty of gel in. In fact if I were you I would gel your arse each morning when you start work."

"But, but, but." Tim stuttered.

"Now go along and put these on your trolley ready for the morning."

Tim knew there no use pleading any more. He picked up the items and said, "Yes Madam. Thank you Madam." And slowly left the room.

Neighbourhood Watch

In one-way Denis and Jill were a good match, Jill was an extrovert and a flirt and Denis was quiet and something of a voyeur. In another way they weren't because they were both submissive. The more obvious traits in their characters got them together and very soon they married.

Denis's promotion took them to a new town and a new house. Jill did not mind giving up her job. For some time she had been wanted to find something, which gave her more opportunity to use her personality.

There was no hurry and with the extra money Denis was now earning she could afford to stay and home for a few weeks and do the necessary redecorations.

It was when she was on the ladder painting in the spare bedroom that she noticed the young lady walking up Joe's drive.

Joe was their next-door neighbour. In his late 50's and semi retired he had been very helpful and despite their age difference Denis and Joe had become friends. For some reason she could not understand Jill was a bit shy with Joe but at the same time she found him sort of attractive.

She watched the girl go into Joe's porch and turned back to her painting. Suddenly she was aware of a movement in Joe's bedroom. From her position on the ladder she had a good view of the room and the bottom half of the double bed. The girl was getting undressed. Jill watched fascinated as she carefully folded up her clothes and then when she was naked she stood by feet together, head bowed and hands clasped behind her.

For a good five minutes nothing happened and then Joe came into view. The girl did not look up or move as Joe examined her. Feeling her bottom and fingering her vagina. Jill was glued to the spot and she was getting very excited. She was suddenly disappointed when Joe disappeared only have a surge of excitement when he reappeared with a hairbrush in his hand. The next moment the girl was over his knee and the back of the brush was coming down across her backside.

Jill nearly fell off the ladder as she orgasmed. She gripped tight as she watched the spanking finish, the girl get up holding her now red bottom and Joe roughly push her over the side of the bed. He kicked her feet apart and the next moment his trousers dropped to his ankles and with one thrust he was in the girl. It was at this moment Jill had her second orgasm and she had her third one when Joe pulled turned and showed her his magnificent organ. Showed her was the correct expression, because he stood holding it and grinning up at her. Clearly he knew she was watching all the time.

Jill did not know what to do with herself for the rest of the day. When Denis got home she dragged him to the bedroom, stripped him and rode him until they both climaxed.

"Whew!" Denis said, "What was that in aid of?"

"That Joe next door." Jill said laying back on the bed and she told Denis in detail what she had witnessed before make further use of his erection caused by her description of the scene.

Later at dinner Denis said, "I suppose you want some of Joe's attention?"

"Bugger his attention, I want some of that lovely cock."

Denis laughed, "Just how are you going to do that then, my little slut."

Jill grinned at him. "Don't worry I don't think it will be much trouble."

The angle of their houses meant that Jill's kitchen window was in full view of Joe's back door and the window on his landing. Jill took off her blouse and bra and started the washing-up. She walked back and forward across the kitchen for what seemed like hours before she saw Joe standing at his landing window grinning at her. She waved.

A few moments later the telephone rang.

"Sorry to disturb you Jill," Joe said, "but I have run out of coffee and I need one."

"Oh Joe, I was just making one, why don't you come over?"

Seconds later, there was a knock on the back door.

Jill just had time to slip on a rather tight nylon blouse that she had put ready, before answering the door.

Joe stepped inside and after slamming the door shut wasted not more time. Grabbing her round the waist with one arm the other had went straight to her breast and started kneading it.

"Why Joe, what are you doing?" Jill said.

"Shut up you little slut, and get this blouse off." Joe growled.

Quickly, but with some difficulty caused by Joe's grip, she did as ordered and then her other breast was being kissed and sucked until she started to gasp for breath.

"Get over that table you bitch," Joe ordered, giving her a push

Jill quickly obeyed.

Joe lifted her loose skirt and threw it over her head. He gave a short whistle when she saw she was not wearing any knickers and her vagina was glistening with juices. He went to kick her legs open but they were already wide so he dropped his jeans and pants and the next moment his rock hard penis was inside Jill. As he thrust in and out Jill started to whimper; "Shut up bitch or you'll get a good spanking." Joe said.

Jill gave a squeal and climaxed just as Joe shot his load up inside her.

With a sigh Joe withdrew and Jill slowly stood up. She stepped over to a cupboard and took out a towel. Joe was still standing with his now slowly sagging erection. Jill carefully cleaned his penis. Then she pulled up his pants and trousers. Joe started to fasten his zip and Jill wiped herself then straightened her dress.

"Coffee?" she said.

"Thanks." Joe replied and sat down at the table.

Jill grinned at Joe as she poured the coffee.

"Well that was nice," Joe said, "but you do realise that I will have you any time I like from now on."

Jill's eyes shone with excitement, "Yes Sir," she said.

Joe took a sip of his coffee. He was thinking hard. Since his divorce some five years before he had been paying local girls to come in about once a month, so he could spank them and treat them a bit rough. Some just did it for the money, but now and again he got the sense that some of them got a genuine thrill from his treatment. This he found quite exciting. Now, he thought, if he played his cards right, he could have a free submissive little whore right next door.

"So you like to be ordered about and have a bit or rough sex then?" he asked.

Jill blushed, "Well yes, I suppose I do."

"And what about David? Does he order you about, and what is he going to say when he finds out I'm fucking you?"

Jill laughed, "Oh I told him all about watching you and that I was going to try and get some of your cock."

"And he did not mind?"

"He was quite excited at the idea and as for ordering me about, he would rather I ordered him."

"I see. Now that is interesting."

"Mind you," Jill added, "he would want to watch."

Joe laughed, "We will have to see about that. Now just how obedient are you?"

"Oh very obedient, Master."

"We will see. You wait here. I will be back."

Jill sat and waited until Joe came back carrying some clothes, which he threw on the table.

"My ex used to work in a canteen. This is one of her uniforms. This one is for doing general cleaning. Not very pretty, but practical. Now if you really want to be my slave you will change into this, no knickers, and report to my front door in uniform ready for work. Is that clear, girl?"

"Yes Sir." Jill said.

"Right you have twenty minutes, if you are not there by then we will forget the whole thing. If you are, then you belong to me to do what I like with."

"Yes Sir."

With that Joe turned and walked out.

The uniform would not have been too bad but it was too big for Jill. The light green overall dress hung round her and she had to find a belt to give it some shape. The tabard just hung and the little soft pillbox type hat was the only thing that fitted. She had to find a suspender belt to she could wear some stockings and a pair of old shoes finished the ensemble.

She wished she could have gone to the back door instead she had to walk up her path and down Joe's and ring the bell in full sight of any watching neighbours. Of course nobody took any notice but she still felt embarrassed.

After a wait of what seemed like hours, Joe opened the door.

"Get in here, girl." He ordered.

Once inside he pushed her into his kitchen.

"Now there is a bit pile of washing up," he said, "do that, clean the kitchen and then scrub the floor. I will be checking on you, so do a good job or you get my belt across your backside."

"Yes Sir." Jill said. She had never considered doing housework as a submissive thing, but having to do it dressed as a servant was somehow exciting, so she immediately got to work.

She was scrubbing the floor when Joe came back into the kitchen. He glanced round.

"Not bad, girl. Keep at it. I may have some guests coming later. What time does Denis get home?"

"About 5.30, Sir."

"Good." Joe said and picked up the wall telephone, he dialled then said, "Harry. It's Joe here. Are you busy this evening?"

"Good, look could you round up three of the lads. Say Bob, Jim and Henry and could you get here about 5.30."

He listened for a while, "Well do your best. I promise you it will be good. I've got a new young slave girl here and I want to give her a good initiation into her sexual duties."

He listened for a few more moments, "Oh yes she's a little cracker and very obedient. Or she will be by the time we have finished with her. Okay, see you then."

Jill could hear this conversation and she was now quite wet with excitement. She stopped scrubbing and was breathing heavily. Joe turned round, "Get on with your work girl and stop listening to conversations that don't concern you. What is your husband's number at work?"

Jill gave his the number including the extension and he dialled it.

"Hallo Denis, this is Joe," he said when he got through, "listen carefully. I have fucked your wife this morning and I might do so again later."

He stopped and listened, "Never mind about all that you just get here by 5 o'clock sharp. I have a surprise for you."

He listened again, "Jill, oh she is okay. She is on her hands and knees scrubbing my kitchen floor. She is trying to do a good job because she knows she will either get my belt across her backside if she doesn't or my cock up her arse if she does. Now you be on time."

Again he listened, "And it's not yes Joe. It's yes Sir, understand?"

"Good."

Jill kept scrubbing. When she finished she had the bed to make, the hall and stairs to clean and after changing in to a cap and apron she had to serve her Master with some refreshments whilst he sat in the lounge watching television. She did not get his belt across her bottom or, to her disappointment, his cock up her arse.

Eventually 5 o'clock came. She had changed in to a waitress uniform, still too big, and laid out some refreshments in the lounge. Sharp at 5 as she was standing in the hall the bell rang and Joe answered it. It was Denis.

"Come in Denis." Joe said.

Denis's eyes widened as he saw his wife standing there.

Joe smiled, "No Denis I have not fucked her again, but she is going to get a good seeing to later. Do you want to watch?

"Do I?" Denis's eyes were shining with excitement, "Of course. What are you going to do to her?"

"You'll find out, but you must do as you're told."

"Of course I will."

"All right then, I am going to tie you to a chair to make sure you don't try and interfere."

Suddenly Denis's already rising erection became rock hard. Something, which was very obvious to Joe.

"I won't interfere, I promise."

"You just said you would do as your were told and you're not doing it."

"I will Joe. I will I promise."

"Right then you get yourself up to my spare bedroom; it's the second door in the right, and strip off. Then stand in the corner facing the wall and wait for me."

Denis hesitated for a second.

"Come on get on with it. Doing as you're told, remember."

Denis nodded his head and said, "Yes of course Joe." And without looking at Jill again started up the stairs.

"Put your clothes neatly in the landing cupboard, then slam the door." Joe called after him.

"Okay Joe."

"And it's Sir to you from now on. Do you understand?"

"Yes Sir." Denis replied and nearly had an orgasm there and then.

Ten minutes later Joe went up the stairs. He opened the self locking landing cupboard door and noted with an nod of satisfaction that Denis's clothes were indeed in there. He shut the door again and went into the bedroom. Denis was standing as he had been ordered.

"Sit in that chair." Joe said.

"Yes Sir." Denis replied and quickly sat in the only chair in the room. It was a heavy chair with strong wooden arms.

Joe opened his wardrobe door and took out a coil of cord. He walked over to Denis and expertly bound him firmly to the chair. Apart from the chair and the wardrobe there was a heavy single bed with iron ends in the middle of the room and a low cupboard. Joe looked round and nodded.

"All ready for your surprise?"

"Yes, thank you Sir."

Joe smiled "Good." He said and went out.

Denis heard the front door bell and the voices as the guests arrived but he could only guess about what was going on. Jill, on the other hand, was taking coats while Joe showed his guests into the lounge. Then Jill served refreshments.

"Okay Joe," Harry said eyeing Jill, "what have you got for us?"

Joe smiled, "What I want to do lads, is to see if we can all come at once."

"What wanking, you mean?" one of them said.

"No this slut here can deal with five cocks at once, and it is she that gets punished if we don't succeed."

"Five? How will she do that?" Harry asked.

"You will find out. She can do a strip while you have your drinks, then we take her upstairs." With that he put some slinky music on the CD player.

"Come on slave, start stripping," he said.

"Yes Sir," Jill replied and started to perform in the best stripper fashion she could. By the time she was naked the lads had finished their drinks.

"Right get up to the spare room girl, and stand by the bed," Joe said, "Now lads you can strip in the main bedroom. Follow me."

Three minutes later the lads trooped into the spare room. Jill was standing by the bed head bowed, legs slightly apart and hands clasped behind. Denis was still tied in the chair.

"Hallo!" Harry asked, "And just who is this?"

Joe laughed, "Oh that's her husband. Never mind about him now. I am about ready."

There was a chorus of, "Me too."

Joe opened the drawer of the bedside cabinet and drew out a little pack of cards.

"You each take one," he said, "number one gets it in her fanny. Number two up her arse. Number three in her mouth and four and five get it in each of her hands.

Bob got the one.

"Right Bob, lie on the bed face up, but well down the bed." Bob took up his position.

Jim had the two and Joe said. Right girl: get on the bed, legs either side of Bob and facing the top then, lower your fanny onto Bob's erection."

Jill did as she was told and Bob groaned as she slid down.

Joe produced a bottle of lubricant and squirted a large quantity up Jill's arse then handed the bottle to Henry.

"Right Jim get up behind her and get up her arse and you two get your cocks greased."

As Jim did so Jill had to bend forward to give him the angle and Bob groaned.

"Hold on Bob." Joe said, "We won't be long. I've got three."

He climbed up over Bob's head and kneeling either side of her, he grabbed Jill's hair and pulled her face to his cock.

"Suck it slut!" He ordered.

Jill was going to anyway and when she did Joe put his arms under her shoulders and took her weight.

"Right you two hurry up, get one each side and get her hands on your cocks."

Supported by Joe Jill was able to grasp a well-lubricated cock in each hand.

"Right slut start wanking and wriggling." Joe ordered and Jill did just that, as eagerly as the rest of them. It was all over in less that two minutes and as far as Joe could tell they had more or less come together in five shuddering climaxes. Jill was covered in cum inside and out as Harry and Henry sprayed her sides, Jim pulled out while still coming and sprayed her back and Joe did the same thing with her head and hair.

They all collapsed on the bed for a few moments Then Joe said, "Right girl, go and get a shower then come back here."

"Yes Sir." Jill said.

Joe handed out towels to the lads to wipe themselves then Jim said, "What about the cuckold here?"

They looked at Denis whose cock was still gently spurting cum.

"The dirty little wimp loved it," Bob said, "What shall we do with him?"

"I tell you what lads," Joe said, "I have got a video camera hidden up there. Once I have blanked out your faces we should have some nice sequences and stills of my little slave and this wimpy husband of hers. Should make a bit of money. Even more if I sold them to his workmates."

Denis's face went white then red and they all laughed.

"No please Sir, don't, you will ruin me."

Joe walked over to him, "You will do as you're told from now on, then?"

"Yes, yes, Sir, anything."

"How do you feel about sucking my cock erect so I can fuck your wife again?"

"Yes please Sir."

Joe turned back to the others, "Right lads, you can do what you like with him. Don't damage him though. I think he is going to be quite valuable."

"What shall we do with him then?" Bob asked.

"Well," Harry said, "knowing Joe I expect he wants to fuck his slut so why don't we have a couple of drinks and a rest then see if we can repeat the experiment with four of us using wimpy boy here."

"Oh yes," Jim said, "how about that, wimp? Would you like one up your arse one in your mouth and one in each hand? Eh!"

Denis looked at the grinning Joe. Actually he did not know if he really had such a video but he could not take a chance and in any case something about the idea of being used like a cheap whore started to get him excited again.

"Oh yes please Sir. Thank you." He said.

They all laughed, just as Jill came back in the room.

"Good," Joe said, "get yourself down to the lounge and serve more drinks, slave."

"Yes Sir." Jill said and went immediately followed by the guests.

Actually at the end of the evening some of the lads thought that Denis was even more enjoyable than Jill had been. Particularly Harry whom Denis sucked off while Henry was fucking his arse. One problem was that Denis was bigger and heavier than Jill so he had to be laid on some pillows to lift his backside and head up while he masturbated Bob and Jim.

The lads were down in the lounge having more drinks when Joe came down after fucking Jill several more times. Bob suggested that Denis should be dressed in Jill's uniform to serve them as a maid.

Jill and Joe had a chuckle as they walked into the lounge to see the lads relaxing with their drinks while Denis in his dress and apron was kneeling between Harry's legs and slowly sucking his cock.

With two maids to attend to them the lads had a few more drinks before taking their leave, after thanking their host for a lovely evening and promising to come again some time.

Joe looked at his two slaves, one naked girl and one partly feminised man.

"Right you two, you can get off home now. You girl, will be here at 8.30 in the morning and bring me my morning tea and give me a blow job if I feel like it."

"Yes Sir," Jill said, "shall I wear my uniform?"

Joe looked thoughtfully and then said, "No I don't think so. It does not fit you very well anyway." He looked Denis up and down and went on. "There are several dresses under the stairs and aprons in that kitchen drawer. You can take them home."

"Yes Sir." Jill said.

"Not you, girl. That pansy wimp there." He walked up to Denis and looked him in the face. "In future Daphne, you will come straight home from work, change into the appropriate uniform, this one will do for tomorrow, and report to me for household duties. Is that clear, girl?"

"Yes Sir." Was all Denis could say.

"Yes Master, from now on, girl."

"Yes, Master."

"Don't forget the video. I do not want to use it but I will if you let me down. "

"Yes Master, I understand."

"Right off you go and don't be late tomorrow."

"Please Sir, I don't have anything to wear." Jill said.

"Well it's dark so you can go as you are."

"Yes Sir."

They turned to go and were just going out of the door when Joe said; "Don't forget you both belong to me now. You are slaves, my slaves and rest assured I am going to make good use of both of you."

"Yes Master." The couple said together as they set off for home with the certain knowledge that their lives had been radically changed and their future was in someone else's hands.

Superior Secretary

Jane was pleased for Madge and pleased she had been invited to stay with her for the summer holidays. She had known Madge from their college days and they had qualified as executive secretaries the same day.

Jane had married her boss but Madge seemed content with her career, which made it more of a surprise when Jane got the letter telling her that Madge had married her boss in Hong Kong. It was only a month of so later that Jane's husband was killed in a plane crash. Madge had flown over to be at the funeral and it was then that she told Jane of their plan to sell the business in Hong Kong and retire to a small estate in England.

As the branch line train drew into the tiny station Jane was looking out of the window and was pleased to see her old friend on the platform. She was still wondering how Madge had hooked such a rich husband. She was no beauty and now in their late 40s the two ladies both looked neat and comfortable rather than smart and sophisticated like many of the wives who moved in their respective social circles.

The ladies hugged while the porter, come stationmaster, come ticket collector collected Jane's baggage from the train and hurried thought the tiny ticket office with it.

"Where is he going with those?" Jane said looking at her friend in her expensive but slightly dowdy country tweeds.

"Oh John will put them in the pony trap. Don't worry."

They strolled past arm in arm as John touched his forelock and took the tip Madge slipped him. They turned the corner into the car park and Jane stopped suddenly in surprise.

There was indeed a pony trap in the car park but between the shafts with it reins tied to the station fence was not a pony but a young lady. Madge pulled on Jane's arm to get her moving again and as they neared the trap Jane could see that the girl was wearing a flesh coloured backless sort of swimming costume, some sort of boots and a head harness. The rein Jane could see was attached to a ring at the side of the girl's mouth, which Jane immediately concluded was on the end of some sort of bit. Madge had not said a word since they left the station building clearly enjoying her friend's surprise.

As Jane got nearer she could see that the girls arms were pulled behind her and strapped along the shafts with her hands gripping some sort of handhold. This forced her to bend forward which exposed her naked back and as they came alongside the trap Jane could see red marks across the girls back which she assumed, correctly as it turned out, were made by the carriage whip which was in a holder. Jane could see that her two bags were now strapped to the back of the pony trap.

"Up you jump my dear and slide over." Madge said cheerfully.

Jane, in somewhat of a daze at the sight she was witnessing, did just that. Madge walked to the front of the trap and untied the reins. Then gripping them she said, "Come on Patty, round you go." And she pulled the girl away from the fence and turned the whole assembly round until the girl was facing towards the entrance to the car park.

She flicked one of the reins over the girl's head, walked back to the trap, stepped up and sat by her friend. Reaching back she pulled a tartan rug from behind her and laid it across their knees tucking it in all round.

"Comfortable?" she said smiling at Jane.

Jane nodded, "Err yes thanks."

"Right." Madge said and she took the whip out of the holder, "Walk on," she ordered and with one had she shook the reins and with the other expertly flicked the whip across the girl's back, making another red line.

The girl immediately started to pull forward, her hands gripping the holds on the shafts and bending over even more to get the now heavy trap started. The trap started to roll on its well-oiled wheels and soon they were out of the car park and moving down the main street of the village.

"Giddy up." Madge ordered and once again the reins shook but this time the whip only cracked over the girl's back. Jane concluded that is was a warning as to what would happen if this girl pony did not respond and quickly.

She did respond as soon they were trotting merrily along, whilst the few people in the street and a couple of shopkeepers at their shop doors smiled, waved or just ignored the spectacle. Jane concluded that it was not a new sight in the village.

Madge slid the whip back in it's holder, "That is an unusual pony Madge." Jane ventured.

"Oh Patty, yes, she is my step-daughter."

"Is she?"

"Yes at first she was very jealous of my relationship with her father, but one day I had had enough of the tantrums and I put her over my knee and took a hair brush to her backside. She could not do enough for me after that."

"Really!"

"Oh yes. I had a Chinese girl who worked as my personal maid in Hong Kong. I told her I wanted Patty trained so that she could do that job when we got back to the UK and that she could use whatever method she liked to train her. You think of these Chinese girls as hard working and they are, but they can relax as well."

"Oh yes?"

"Yes within two weeks she was doing nothing but supervising Patty. She even made her wear a maid's uniform while she wore a smart dress."

"What did your husband think about this?"

"He was a bit ambivalent about it," Madge laughed, "it was one of his uniforms."

They were now out of the village and approaching the gates of a large house standing in it's own grounds. Patty was beginning to breathe hard as she had been trotting for over a mile pulling quite a load.

"Your pony's getting tired, Madge."

"Yes, she needs more exercise. I think less fussing about with my undies and more time in the shafts will improve her. Maybe you could help me with that while you're here. In the mean time we had better take some action."

She pulled the whip out of it's holder and, 'Swish! Crack!'. It came down across the girl's back once, twice, three times in quick succession.

"Get up you lazy mare." Madge shouted and the girl immediately started to move faster into what was almost a gallop.

It was only few yards before Madge pulled on the reins. "Whoa!" she said and the girl slowed down before Madge pulling on the left hand rein guided her through the gates of the big house.

In a few moments they had pulled up in front of the house and Madge jumped down. Her cheeks were flushed and she had clearly enjoyed the drive as indeed had Jane. She quickly hitched the reins to a rail by the front door as a person in a blue and white striped dress with a plain bibbed apron over it and a plain maid's cap on it's head came down the front steps.

"There you are Harry. Say hallo to Jane."

Jane immediately recognised Madge's husband.

He held the sides of his apron and curtsied. "Nice to see you again Madam." He said.

"Now Harry you can carry Jane's bags to her room. Tell Mrs Wood we will have tea in the lounge. You can serve it."

"Yes Madam." Harry said as he un-strapped the bags.

"After tea you can unpack for Jane. Where is Tom?"

"In the yard, Madam."

"Good we'll go round. Oh, by the way you will be looking after Jane and myself for while."

"Yes Madam." Harry said with a smile.

"Don't think that is going to get you out of working for Mrs Wood, my girl."

Harry's face dropped, "No Madam of course not."

"It just means you will find out what being a maid-servant is really all about."

"Yes Madam." Harry replied as we went in with Jane's bags.

Madge untied Patty's reins. "Come and meet Tom." She said to Jane. He is my handy man, come gardener, come stable hand. Early forties, divorced and a bit of a dish."

She laughed as she led her pony and carriage round the side of the house into a stable yard where a man was painting one of the doors.

"Hallo Tom. This is my friend Jane."

"Pleased to me you." Tom said offering his hand

"Now Tom." Madge went on "Patty was blowing a bit coming back from the station. I am going to put her back in harness for a few weeks. I want her exercised every day. I'm sure Jane will give us a hand."

"I certainly will." Jane said.

"Could you give her a rub down and stable her for me? I'll have Mrs Woods prepare her special food."

"Of course Madge. I would be only too pleased. Leave her with me."

Madge took Jane's arm and ushered her towards the back door, "Come on my dear. I will get our maid to show you to your room so you can freshen up. Then we will have some tea. I do hope you are going to enjoy your stay."

"Oh, my dear," Jane said, "You don't have to worry on that score."

Tenancy Agreement

It had been the solicitor's idea. As he had pointed out to David, with the legacy his aunty had left he could afford to live in the garden flat in the semi-basement and let the rest of the house. It meant giving up his job, but once he had got the place straight and let then he could look for another job. However the place had to be put in order first. He was looking forward to that. Up to now he had only worn his various maid's uniforms to clean his little flat. Now there was the garden flat, the utility room and the five-bed room Victorian house upstairs. Most of it had not been used or cleaned for over ten years.

It was two months hard work but it gave him a wonderful excuse to go out and buy different overall dresses, tabards, caps and aprons. By the end of the second week he did not care if neighbours saw him hanging out his dresses and undies on the line. If they did see him they would only think he was a cleaning lady employed to get the place straight.

Eventually it was done and David had just hung yesterday's dress, tabard and cap plus his undies when he heard the phone. It was his solicitor.

"Hallo David. How is the cleaning going?"

"Just finished."

"Are you interested in a let?"

"Of course."

"I have my cousin with me. Her husband has been moved into one of the local banks to sort out some problems and they need a place to rent."

"It's a bit big for two."

"They've got two teenage girls as well. They are going to let their place in London. Your house will be ideal."

"Well okay, when can they come and look?"

"I'll send her round right away. Should be there in twenty minutes or so."

"Okay." David said and put the phone down.

He looked in the mirror and saw a domestic cleaner staring back at him.

"Whoops, I had better get changed." He said to his mirror image.

David was a little surprised when a coloured lady, who he could only describe as statuesque, stood on the doorstep.

"I am Lorna Harris." she said, "My cousin sent me to see the house."

David was so taken with her appearance that he had forgotten his manners.

"Oh yes, yes please." He said and almost bowed as he ushered her in and started to show her round.

They were standing in the lounge by the large window that overlooked the garden when Mrs Harris said, "I like it. It is very smart and clean. My cousin told me it was in a bit of a mess. Who cleaned it?"

David was so pleased with the compliment that he said, "Oh, I did."

Mrs Harris looked out of the window and turned back smiling, "You would not be kidding me would you?"

"Oh no, Mrs Harris. I can assure you I have been working on the place for over six weeks all alone. I only finished this morning."

"Well, your wife must be pleased with you."

"I'm not married. I live on my own."

Mrs Harris nodded and with another glance in the garden she said, "I see, in that case we'll take it. Now I do have a problem, which you may be able to help me with."

"If I can."

"I am a legal secretary and a local agency say they can soon find me a job. The girls are at college and this is a big house. I will need a cleaner five mornings during the week. Could you advise me on that?"

She turned and looked out of the window again, "Well I have only been in the town since I inherited the house, about eight weeks, and I don't know many people."

She looked him up and down, "My cousin tells me you gave up your job when you came here."

"Yes Mrs Harris."

"So you are not doing anything at the moment?"

"That's right, Mrs Harris."

"Well I can see you are very good at cleaning and you live right downstairs. Why don't you take the job on?"

"Oh! Well I am not sure. I don't know what I could charge."

She gave David a smile that made him go weak at the knees and said, "I'm not sure myself. I tell you what why don't you try it for a couple of weeks and then we will discuss it and decided."

"Yes, all right Mrs Harris."

"Good. I will probably be around for the first few days and I can tell you how I want things done. Then the second week you can be on your own and see how you like it."

"Yes, Mrs Harris."

"That is settled then. We will move in over the weekend and you can start on Monday."

David was both happy and apprehensive. It was all very well doing housework for himself but would he be able to satisfy Mrs Harris? He wandered back into the lounge and looked at the garden to see what had been interesting Mrs Harris. On the line were his uniform plus two of his corselets and a matching slip and knickers. He had told her he lived alone.

It was in some trepidation that David knocked on the back door that Monday. Mrs Harris opened it with a smile, "Right on time," Mrs Harris said, "I like that. Come in."

David stepped inside as Mrs Harris went on, "I do have one question. I can't see a washing machine?"

"Oh I'm sorry. I should have shown you. There is a utility room at the bottom of the back staircase. That is how you get into my flat from the garden."

"Oh good, show me."

Mrs Harris looked round the room and noted the large washing machine, drier, ironing board and the rotary press.

"This is very good," she said, "you will be able to do all our laundry in here."

David was startled. He had not anticipated doing laundry for five people, but he could not say no to this woman. The next second it occurred to him that there would be lots of exciting undies to handle, so he said, "Oh yes, Mrs Harris," which made her smile again.

Then David's heart gave a jump as she walked to the large cupboards, which lined the end wall.

"What's in these?"

"Oh, the boiler, airing cupboard and cleaning things." He said quickly and before he could say any more she had swung open two of the doors. One had the boiler and shelves in it but the other had a hanging rail with David's uniforms hanging in plain sight.

With no comment she shut the doors and opened the one with the cleaning tools. Then shutting this she said, "Well we had better put you to work," she looked him up and down. "Don't you have some sort of protective clothing to wear. You will get your shirt and trousers very dirty."

"Err! Well yes. I do have a tabard."

"I suggest you get it on and some sort of hat too, and do come on, David, there is a lot of work to do."

With that she walked out of the door leaving David to hurry to the cupboard. He slipped the tabard on with practised ease, even though his hands were shaking. The matching headscarf was a bit more difficult but he managed it. When he was back in Mrs Harris's kitchen she was standing tapping her foot.

"At last," she said, "first clear the breakfast things, wash up and clean the kitchen. That will be your first task every morning. Then make the beds and tidy the bedrooms. I will work out a schedule for you. A different room or rooms every day. I will be in the lounge if you need me. Report to me when you have finished the kitchen and I will inspect your work." With that she walked out of the door.

David could not believe it. Her manner had changed abruptly from friendly ease to an air of total authority and it left him in a sort of trance for a second or two. He shook his head to clear it and started work.

An hour later Mrs Harris was showing him how she wanted the beds made.

"Pick up any clothes lying about. Underwear you put in the wash. Outer clothing you will examine. If it needs cleaning put that in the wash or take it to the cleaners. If in doubt, ask."

"Yes Mrs Harris."

"The girls and I like our jeans with the creases down the sides. My husband likes his down the front. Oh and put his shirts and our blouses in hangers."

"Yes, Mrs Harris."

It was well into the afternoon before David had finished. As he left to go back to his flat carrying the dirty laundry Mrs Harris handed him a note, "This is your schedule David. I will see you at nine in the morning. Don't be late."

"Thank you Mrs Harris. I won't be." David said, glad that the washing held in front of him was hiding the erection her words were causing.

Once in his flat he looked at the paper.

Mon: Wash up. Do the weekend's washing up; give the kitchen a thorough clean. Make beds. Tidy bedrooms.

Tues: Wash up. Clean kitchen. Make beds and tidy bedrooms. Thoroughly clean hall, landings and stairs.

Weds: Wash up. Clean kitchen. Make beds and tidy bedrooms. Thoroughly clean lounge and dining room.

Thurs: Wash up. Clean kitchen. Make beds and tidy bedrooms. Thoroughly clean bathrooms and toilets.

Fri: Wash up. Clean kitchen. Clean linen on all beds. Thoroughly clean all bedrooms.

David could not believe it. This was not part time, it would take him most of the day and what about the laundry she expected him to do? He went back upstairs and knocked on the door.

"Please Mrs Harris this schedule. It will take me most of every day to do this."

She smiled at him, "Yes David at first, but once you are used to it you should be finished by one or two in the afternoon."

"But you also want me to do the laundry as well."

"Of course, but you have all weekend and evenings. Well at least, at the moment," she patted his cheek and her smile went even wider, "now don't you worry. I will be very tolerant at first and if you can't manage you can finish off on Saturday morning. Off you go now."

How did you resist such a woman? David went back to his flat in a daze.

The rest of the week was like a sort of dream. He just worked and worked while Mrs Harris went about her business, only occasionally inspecting his work and commenting on the standard, but eventually Friday came and he was standing in the kitchen with a big bag of dirty sheets. Determined to tell Mrs Harris that he could not carry on working like this.

"I am quite pleased with you David," she said and she put one hand on his shoulder, "however at times you seemed all hot and bothered. I think you would be better to wear something more suitable, something a bit cooler. I could not help but notice in your cupboard that you had some suitable attire. I won't object if next week you want to wear something like that."

David forgot everything he wanted to say, "You mean you don't mind?"

She laughed, "Of course not, but I would like you to look presentable. You know hair done nicely and a touch of make up."

"Thank you Mrs Harris," David gushed as he picking up the bag of dirty laundry.

Monday morning David appeared in his green Alexandra's dress with the wrap-round apron and a matching hat. His black court shoes gleamed. He had been out at the weekend and bought some heated curlers so his hair was laid in neat curls. His face was lightly creamed and powdered and he wore a pale lipstick.

"Well!" Mrs Harris said, "You do look nice, but I can't call you David. What would you like to be called?"

"Daphne, please Mrs Harris."

"Okay. Daphne it is and you can call me Madam."

Maybe it was because he had had some practise or maybe it was wearing the uniform but David's day seemed to go like clockwork. He sailed through the work.

"There you are you silly girl," his Mistress said, "despite all that washing up you have finished over an hour earlier than last week. It was just a matter of putting your mind to it."

"Yes, thank you Madam."

"Now I am starting a new job tomorrow, so you will be on your own. I want you to start at 8.30 so I can give you any special instructions before I go to work."

"Of course, Madam." David said as he left carrying the weekend's dirty laundry.

David spent a really happy week. A lot of work, of course, but a different uniform every day and a chance to try some of Mrs Harris's pretty dresses on.

Friday evening Mrs Harris knocked on David's door, "I think we had better have a meeting in the morning," she said, "about 10.30?"

David agreed of course, but he did not sleep very well that night wondering what would be said, or if Mrs Harris had found out about him trying her clothes on.

Sharp at 10.30 he was there. The whole family were sitting in the lounge and David was directed to stand in front of them.

"We have had a family meeting," Mrs Harris said, " In general we are all happy with your work."

"Thank you." David said.

"Please don't interrupt me."

"Sorry, Madam."

Mrs Harris went on, "We are all aware of how you like to dress when you're working and we are all happy about that. However there will be times when you are working and we have visitors. In such a case we expect you to carry on with your work unless you are given permission to stop. Is that clear?"

Immediately David could visualise what might happen. Miss Helen was 17 and Miss Wendy 15 so in the holidays there could be teenage girls walking around. It could be very embarrassing, but there was no way he could stop now.

"Yes, Madam, quite clear."

"And you still wish to continue working in uniform?"

"Yes please, Madam."

"I understand that you do not need to do this work for money. Is that right?"

"Well yes Madam, although I do have expenses. Make-up, new uniforms, cleaning materials."

"Yes that is true. Here is what we propose. We will cover any expenses but we will not pay you for doing the work. What have you to say about that?"

"Nothing Madam, if that is your decision I am not in a position to argue."

"Good. However my husband suggested that what you get out of doing this is working, dressing and being treated as a woman, which we assume you like."

She looked expectantly at him, "Oh yes, Madam."

"Now since you will work mostly on your own there will be nobody to see you or treat you as a woman, so as a sort of payment for your work we are going to allow you to return each evening wearing one of your more formal black and white uniforms, when you will be our parlour maid. Does that sound nice for you?"

David had this vivid picture of him in his black dress with the frilly white collar, white cap and apron serving tea and coffee and it felt marvellous.

"Oh yes, Madam."

"Good, then starting Monday you will be here at 6.30 to assist me in laying the table. You will then serve dinner. You will serve coffee in the lounge after and you will clear and wash-up. That will save you some time the next morning. Won't it?"

"Oh yes, Madam, thank you."

"Now what time you leave in the evenings will be up to us. We may make you stand in the hall in case we need you later or we may dismiss you straight after you have cleared up. Is that clear?"

"Oh yes, Madam, crystal clear."

"And you accept the position with the conditions?"

"Yes please, Madam."

Mrs Harris turned to her husband, "You were quite right dear she is a natural slave," then turning back to her new maid she said, "You can go now Daphne. Be here sharp 8.30 on Monday."

David could hardly believe it. Two weeks ago he had played around dressing as a maid from time to time. Then he was a cleaner or daily woman and now he was to be a proper maid. It was all going rather fast but he could not stop.

Six o'clock David was standing dressed in a Simon Jersey waitress uniform with it's neat pointed apron and matching hat waiting for the time to report for his new duties. The clock seemed to crawl round but eventually he mounted the stairs at the back of the house and knocked on the back door. As he got to the top of the stairs he was conscious of the lady next door standing in her garden and watching him.

He stood there not daring to look round for two long minutes before Miss Helen opened the door.

"Oh Daphne, you could have come in the door was open," she said.

Mrs Harris was just behind her smiling. "Now that looks very smart Daphne. Come on, I am just laying the table."

As far as David was concerned the evening was a disaster. He was so nervous he dropped several items of cutlery, and although he did not actually drop a dinner plate he did scatter potatoes across the kitchen floor and managed to spill the wine.

The final straw was handing Mr Harris a cup of coffee with it spilt in the saucer.

When he had finished clearing and washing-up he reported back to the lounge as ordered. The girls had gone out but Mr and Mrs Harris were having a drink.

"Well Daphne, it was not very good was it?" his Mistress said.

"No Madam. I am sorry, please let me carry on. I will try to do better."

"We have been discussing the situation and we decided that you were nervous and of course inexperienced, so we are going to overlook tonight's faults."

David breathed a sigh of relief.

"However it is clear you need training and with that goes discipline. Now there are things we can do. You can be made to stand in a corner for an hour or so but that is a waste of time. You can of course be dismissed, but we feel that you will be useful in time. What we need is something that is quick, immediate and something you won't forget. Have you got any ideas?"

David thought he knew what she was driving at so he said, "You could give me a spanking, Madam."

The Harrises raised their eyebrows and looked at each other, Mrs Harris said, "A spanking Jeff? What do you think?"

"Huh! A spanking? What she needs is a dose of the strap."

"Well Daphne, you heard the Master. He thinks you need the strap. You know what that means, don't you?"

"Yes, Madam." David said going pale.

"Well, what do you think? Would that help you?"

"I don't know, Madam."

"You don't, eh. Well I think it is worth a try. We will get one during the week and hang it in the kitchen where it will remind you to take more care. Now go and stand in the hall facing the wall and think about how you are going to do to avoid making careless errors in the future."

With a curtsey, David left the room and took up his position as ordered. As he stood there he realised that what he thought had been a disastrous evening was not so bad. He had not been dismissed, he was not going to be punished and he only had to be more careful in the future. Two hours later he was still standing there with an erection like a rod of iron and very sticky knickers. Both Mr and Mrs Harris had come through the hall a couple of times and Miss Wendy had returned but they had all ignored him as though he was a piece of furniture. He was wondering what Miss Helen might say when she returned but before that happened his Mistress came into the hall and said, "All right Daphne, you may go home now but don't be late in the morning."

"David turned and curtsied," thank you Madam," he said and without thinking went to the front door.

"Servants use the back door," Mrs Harris said, "that will be two strokes of the strap when we get it."

David curtsied again, and went to the back door, thinking that it might not be as easy as he thought to avoid punishment.

Tuesday went much better; David was more confident and the dinner went smoothly. He did manage to break a cup when he was washing up, which he reported to Mrs Harris when he finished that evening.

"I see," she said, "that will be two more strokes of the strap."

"But Madam, they are my cups. I will replace it."

Mrs Harris's face was like thunder, " Are you presuming to argue with me, girl? Of course you will replace it, but it is still carelessness and none of us want that in a maid. That will be two more strokes for questioning my decision."

"Yes, Madam."

"Now go and stand in the hall facing the wall."

"Yes, Madam."

It was Friday when David started to serve the meal and saw a two-fingered tawse lying on the table.

Mr Harris saw him looking at it, "Yes Daphne, I put tawse in the search engine and it gave me a site with lots of punishment items. I will give you the bill. It is, after all, household equipment. Every rented house or flat should have one in the kitchen." And the whole family laughed.

The strap stayed there all the time David was serving. Eventually the family got up from the table. David, having served the sweet, was standing by the wall with his hands neatly clasped in front of his apron.

"I think you should have your punishment before coffee, Daphne," his Mistress said, "go and bend over the kitchen table, skirts up, knickers down."

"Yes, Madam." David replied and set off for the kitchen.

"Can we watch, Mummy?" Helen asked.

"Watch!" Wendy burst out "I want to do it."

Mrs Harris looked at her husband who shrugged, "Well I suppose they will have to learn some time."

Poor David not only did he have the humiliation of being punished on his bare bottom, it was done in full sight of the females of the family and the youngest member carried it out. It should have been easier on him, but Wendy was a very keen tennis player and he received three very hard strokes of the strap on each buttock. It was with tears in his eyes that he curtsied to his Mistress and her two daughters and thanked them for his punishment.

"Hang the strap on the back of the broom cupboard door with the rest of the household equipment." His Mistress said.

Much to David's relief and to Miss Wendy's disappointment there was very little excuse to use the strap for the next few months and David settled down into a routine of housework and serving duties for the Harrises, and at the same time dealing with his own affairs. One evening he asked permission to speak to Mr Harris and get some advise about his investments. From then on Mr Harris took a keen interest and his help and advice increased David's assets considerably.

One evening as David was serving the coffee Mrs Harris said, "It is Helen's 18th birthday shortly and we planned to give her a big party."

"Yes, Madam."

"It will be a Saturday evening and there will be the lady next door and some family members apart from friends. You may help me get things ready and then serve as a maid at the party."

"But Madam, what will your family and the neighbours say when they see me?"

Mrs Harris laughed, "I don't know but I think you should have a new uniform. A copy of a Victorian one would be nice. Also I have had a word with my hairdresser. They are beauticians as well and they are willing to give you a good makeover that morning. I think you will look very nice. Of course our neighbour knows about you anyway, because I explained to her why there appeared to be two people living in your flat. I have also explained to my mother about you and she approves. Your Master's parents are dead and any other family members will just have to put up with it. Now you will work this weekend and get the spare room ready for my mother. I don't mind when you do it, but she is coming in Monday."

"Yes, Madam."

As far as David was concerned this was all too wonderful for words. A party to serve at, a make over, plus another lady to serve.

Mrs Harris's mother was in her sixties but still a good-looking woman and Jamaican born and bred.

David was doing his housework when the taxi arrived with her. As she stepped inside the door she looked him up and down.

"So you're the white boy my daughter is using as a maid."

"Yes, Madam."

She suddenly chuckled and as David stood there she walked round him and stood in front of him nodding as if in approval, "You call me Madam Lewis."

"Yes, Madam Lewis."

"Now you work hard, be obedient and respectful of your betters and we gonna get on."

"Yes, Madam Lewis."

"Actually Daphne that is not my words. That was said to me when I first came to England and got a job as a housemaid. However it applies to you and now you know that I know all the little tricks you maidservants can get up to."

David knew then he was going to like this lady, "Yes, Madam Lewis," he said and this time he curtsied.

Mrs Lewis chuckled again, "Oh very nice Daphne. Now I will have coffee and biscuits in the lounge and whilst I am having it, you can take my luggage up to my room and unpack for me."

"Yes, Madam Lewis, but I have never been taught how to be a lady's maid."

She patted his cheek, "Don't worry Daphne. My daughter tells me that she keeps a punishment strap in the kitchen."

"Yes, Madam Lewis."

"Well, you will soon learn then, won't you?"

"Yes, Madam Lewis."

David enjoyed unpacking for Madam Lewis. She had nice dresses and some old fashioned but very sexy undies. He put everything away carefully and reported back to her.

"I'll inspect later," she said, "anything wrong and I'll punish you this evening."

"Yes, Madam Lewis."

She smiled at him, "You know I had my doubts when my daughter told me she had a man as a maid but I think I am going to enjoy ordering you about. Now you can get on with your work."

It was a week until the party and there was a lot to do. David had even more to do because he was working for an extra hour every day so that he could attend to Mrs Lewis. He was wondering if he could ask her if he could go and live with her and be her maid full time but he realised it was a silly idea as Mrs Harris would never allow it.

David was both nervous and excited about the party but although he enjoyed it, taking coats, serving drinks and refreshments, very little attention was paid to him. One or two guests commented on his smart uniform and the next-door neighbour told him how she had asked Mrs Harris if she could employ him as a cleaner, only to be told he was too busy but apart from that he was mostly ignored. He soon realised that this was right, as he was, after all, only the servant. The real shock came the next day. He had managed to get a few hours sleep before changing into his morning uniform to start clearing up the mess. He was well into that when Mrs Harris rang the servant's bell, which she kept by her bed.

"We will have tea in bed Daphne," she said, "and as it is rather late we will skip breakfast. Prepare us a light lunch and serve it in the dining room in an hour."

"Yes, Madam." David replied and thought he had better not remind her that he did not work on Sundays.

The whole family were at lunch and as David was pouring then tea and serving it Mrs Harris said

"Now Daphne we have been discussing your future."

"Oh yes, Madam."

"As you may know Madam Lewis has recently retired from her position as a senior housekeeper in a London hotel."

"Yes Madam, she did tell me."

"Good. Now her problem is that she lived in so she has to find somewhere to live. She has expressed a wish to live near us and it occurred to me that your flat would be ideal for her."

The thought came into David's head immediately of Madam Lewis sitting in his lounge with him waiting on her, "Yes Madam but where would I live?"

Mrs Harris smiled, Mr Harris gave a chuckle and the others were all grinning at him.

"Now that is the beauty of the idea Daphne. You can move into the guest bedroom."

"I see, Madam." David said a bit hesitantly.

"Don't you see you would be our full time live in maidservant. Instead of paying rent mother has agreed to take over the running of the house and would therefore be in charge of you. I think you will agree she is fully qualified for that little task."

"Well yes, Madam. May I think about that?"

Mrs Harris's smile faded, "No you may not. I was not asking you, you stupid girl. I was telling you. We will do the change around today."

"Yes, Madam." David said, and he knew then his fate was sealed.

As he said this Mrs Lewis got up and smiling broadly as she came up to David. She patted him on the cheek and said, "Now Daphne don't you think it is going to be just wonderful. You can look after me and I will complete your training so you will be a servile, obedient and very feminine house maid."

What could David say but, "Yes Madam Lewis. Shall I clear away now?"

"In a moment," his Mistress said, "there is one other thing. Mr Harris has been looking after your affairs for the past couple of months. As he is now to stay at the bank permanently he feels it would be better if he took full control. We have a power of attorney here. You can sign it now and then all you have to worry about it serving us. Mother and Helen can witness it. Here is a pen."

With a sigh of resignation David signed himself into his new life.

The Colonial Convert

I have been around "The Scene" for many years now and like to keep up with the latest events. So when I heard about a new bar opening with some interesting aspects I decided to investigate. It was in a city the name of which is unimportant and owned by a gentleman of African descent who I'd ran into from time to time. It promised topless transsexual waitresses, which sounded intriguing. Discreet it certainly was. First to the top floor of a large office building and then, if your face fitted you took one of two lifts to the penthouse. No doubt there were stairs but they were not obvious.

It was a good evening and the owner, lets call him 'Winston', made sure I was kept happy by a very pretty waitress.

"No doubt," he said with a grin, "You'd like to be waiting on the guests John, but you're not pretty enough. I may find you a job washing up if you like, in uniform of course." And he went off chuckling to himself.

Actually as far as I was concerned it was a proposition to be considered. At least for the few days I was to spend in that city.

It was in the early hours of the morning that I went to step into the lift. The staff were leaving and in front of me was a woman who from her clothing I took to be a cleaner.

She stepped aside for me, but I ushered her in and the two of us started down. The lift stopped with a bump. We stood for a few moments and then the cleaner picked up the emergency telephone and pushed a button.

We were stuck. They needed a lift engineer, it was 4 o'clock in the morning and we were told that it would be at least an hour and maybe three.

We settled down and I took a good look at my companion. Her voice was rather deep for a woman but I have met women with deeper ones, she was in her 60's and she said her name was Jenny.

"I am the toilet cleaner." She said.

"Men's or Ladies?" I asked with a laugh.

"Both," she said, "I am a man, of a sort, but I am always dressed as a woman."

As you can imagine I was very interested.

"How long have you worked for Winston then?"

"I don't work for him. He owns me."

"Owns you, how come?"

"Well he bought me, that's how come."

"No. I mean how did it all happen?"

"You don't want to know all that?"

"Oh yes I do, my dear. I'm thinking of taking a job as a kitchen maid with Winston for a few days. Unpaid of course."

She stared at me for a moment, "I'd keep clear of him if I were you," she said. Then she shrugged her shoulders, "Who am I to talk." She sat down on the floor and said, "I suppose we've got a couple of hours so you might as well know."

I sat down opposite her, "Go on then. Tell me." And this is her story as she told it:
-

I suppose I was one of the last of the colonials. I got this job in an African country a few months before they Africanised the civil service. I had a villa and three servants. There was Paul who was the son of a chief from a tribe further into the interior of the country. He had spent several years in England and had married an English girl of West Indian stock called Wendy, who was my housemaid and then there was my cook Rachel, who despite her Western name was Paul's second wife from his tribe. I was not familiar with the customs and I knew Rachel was Paul's wife because they lived in a hut at the end of my garden but I thought Wendy was single as she slept in the house. Had I know the real situation I might never have done what I did. She paused for a moment. I don't know, I suppose I would have eventually.

Wendy just did her work in ordinary western clothes but this was not good enough for me. I ordered her some really nice uniforms. Some for cleaning, some for general serving duties and a long Victorian style one for waiting at table. She seemed delighted with them. When they arrived we were alone in the house. I had had a few drinks and Wendy was going in and out of the room showing off her uniforms. In the end I could not stand it any more.

"Let me try one on Wendy." I said; I have to tell you I did have several items of female underclothing but because Wendy did my washing I had not been wearing them. They were locked away in a suitcase in my room; or so I thought.

She looked at me and then laughed "Which one, Master?"

"The evening one," I said, "with the long skirt."

For a moment she hesitated, and then she said, "Oh no. You will wear the cleaning uniform and then I can get you to do some cleaning. Are you going to wear proper undies?"

I had an immediate and raging erection. I half gasped and half whispered, "I think so Wendy. Do you mind?"

"Oh no." she said "I will lay it all out on your bed. You finish your drink and then come to the bedroom."

I do not know how I was able to sit and finish that drink so calmly. Eventually I got up and went into the bedroom. Wendy was not there, but on the bed was the blue and white striped dress with the plain-bibbed apron and kitchen maid's cap that I had chosen for her and beside it was a set of my own undies. She clearly had a key to the suitcase and knew about them. As I was changing I noticed she had placed on my dressing table some items of make-up. I had not had a lot of practise, only with my mother's when she was out, but I did my best. When I was ready I looked at myself in the mirror. I thought I made quite a good-looking housemaid. I took a deep breath and went to the kitchen.

Wendy was standing by the window as I stepped in the door and curtsied.

"About time too, you lazy slut," she said, *"now I want all this washing-up done and then you can clean the walls and surfaces and scrub the floor."*

"Yes Miss." I said.

She took three steps towards me, which brought her face close to mine.

"It's Madam to you, slut, and don't you ever forget to curtsey to me again."

And she brought her hand up and gave me a slap across the face which made my eyes water.

It was wonderful. For the first time I was living one of my favourite fantasies, a female domestic servant to a strict Mistress.

A couple of times Wendy came back into the kitchen to see if I was working properly. She had changed into her best dress and was carrying a cane, which she had cut from the garden. I was in a state of ecstasy.

I heard her put my record player on and assumed she was taking it easy in the lounge while I did her work. I did not know how right I was because when I eventfully finished and went to the lounge to report it was not just Wendy. Paul was sitting there drinking one of my beers, his white teeth gleaming as he grinned at me. There was no question of any sort of blackmail. I knew, and those two knew, I could not resist repeating the experience I had just had.

"Your maid looks a bit of a mess, Wendy," Paul said, *"What's her name?"*

I blushed because I knew that I was all sweaty and my apron was dirty.

"Her name's Jenny and you're right. How dare you come in here is such a state, girl," she said as she got up, swinging her cane, *"get back in that kitchen and bend over the table."*

I was aware as I lay across the kitchen table of Paul leaning in the doorway as he watched Wendy give me ten strokes of the cane across my newly bared buttocks.

"Now get changed into your afternoon uniform and report to me in the lounge." Wendy ordered.

When I reported as ordered there was no sign of Wendy. Paul was sitting in my armchair with my newspaper on his lap.

"Your Mistress has gone out," he said, *"come over here."*

I walked over and stood in front of him, then curtsied.

"I was coming to tell you that I take over your job at the end of next month."

I was expecting something like that anyway, because I had recommended Paul for the job.

"Thank you, Sir." I said and curtsied again.

Paul smiled, *"For the rest of the time you are here you will do as you are told. Is that clear, girl?"*

"Yes Sir."

"Your Mistress and my other wife will be out for at least a couple of hours. Now girl, just you look what the sight of you in your pretty uniform has done to me." He threw the newspaper to one side to reveal a large, black and very erect penis.

I gulped and I am sure I went a little white because I knew what was coming and I did not think that I could resist.

"Sorry Sir." I said.

"Sorry! Sorry!" he replied "Too late to be sorry, my girl. Get on your knees and deal with it."

That was the first time I had ever sucked cock. I knelt down between his spread legs and taking his penis in one hand, I applied my lips to the end. His hands gripped my hair. "Get sucking you tart." He said and forced my head down.

It did not take long, only about three or four sucks and his semen was gushing out into my throat.

"Swallow it all, girl," he said, "unless you want me to give you the cane."

For the next few days we went to the office together but once Paul had decided he could cope he told me that I could spend the rest of my time working as his housemaid.

He and Rachel moved into my rooms. Wendy moved into the guest rooms and I moved into Wendy's room at the back of the kitchen. As far as I know, Wendy never did wear those uniforms again but I did every day and both she and Rachel proved to be very strict but also very good Mistresses. For the last two weeks I was dressed only as a maid even when Paul invited his friends and work colleagues home for drinks or a meal. Most of them found it very amusing to have a white man waiting on them as a maid.

I believe Paul was considering keeping me there as a maid after my contract was finished but I think that his new boss advised against it. So the day came when I was permitted to put my male clothes back on and all three of them took me to the airport.

"Do you have anywhere to go when you get back?" Paul said.

"No not really, I'll find some digs and then look for a job."

At that moment my flight was called and I left.

As I came out of the gate at Heathrow and a black lady came up to me.

"Mr Green?" she asked.

When I acknowledged that I was she said, "I'm Mrs Johnson, Wendy's sister. Paul asked me to meet you. I've got the car in the car park."

As we went to her car I was thinking how kind it was of Paul to get her to meet me. No doubt it was some sort of reward for him using me as his concubine for the last six weeks.

Mrs Johnson was somewhat older than Wendy but still a good-looking woman. I never did find out about Mr Johnson. It only took about twenty minutes to get to her house. We went in by the side door into a large kitchen. There was a white girl there dressed in a domestic uniform.

"This is my maid Jane." Mrs Johnson said "You're a bit late for dinner but Jane has saved you something."

I sat at the kitchen table and ate while Mrs Johnson sat drinking a glass of wine and chatting. I found out I was in a guesthouse and she wanted to know about me, and what my plans were. I had several glasses of wine myself and then suddenly I felt very tired. Mrs Johnson showed me to a small room and said goodnight. I stripped and fell into bed.

The next morning I woke up as fresh as a daisy. There was no sign of my bag or my clothes except for some female undies I had brought back. Hung on the door was a blue nurses dress and on the dressing table my make-up was laid out.

It was clear that Mrs Johnson wanted me dressed as a woman. In any case I needed the loo urgently and had no choice but to put the dress on. As I went carefully down the stairs I could hear chattering coming from the dining room. I hurried to the kitchen where Mrs Johnson and Jane were preparing and serving breakfasts.

"There you are at last," Mrs Johnson said, "get that apron on and start washing those pots."

I hurried to obey. This was just great, as far as I was concerned.

Half an hour later the breakfasts were finished and between us Jane and I cleared up while Mrs Johnson sat and drank a coffee.

When we were done Jane said, "Finished Madam."

"Right. You girls can have your breakfast while I get changed. Then I'll deal with Jenny here."

As we ate I said to Jane. "What is she going to do with me?"

She looked me up and down, "Anything she likes, by the look of you."

We had just finished when Mrs Johnson came back.

"I have to take Jenny somewhere Jane. Look after things for me. I'll be back before we have to get dinner ready."

"Yes Mrs Johnson." Jane said grinning at me, "I hope she enjoys it."

"Never mind about that. Take that apron off Jane, and come here."

I did that and went over to her. I could see she had a pair of handcuffs in her hand.

"Turn round and hands behind you." She ordered. I knew she was going to handcuff me but I could not resist and a moment later it was done.

"Come on." She said and taking my arm pushed me into the hall.

There were guests coming and going up and down the stairs but I just had to stand there hands cuffed behind me and trying to hide as much as possible. Mrs Johnson was rummaging in a cupboard under the stairs. Then she put a dark blue plastic rain cape over my shoulders. She spun me round, buttoned it up and pulled the hood up. The fact that it was a rather fine day did not help my embarrassment as she ushered me out of the door to her car.

A few minutes later I was sitting in a car and she was driving me into London.

"Please Madam. Where are we going?" I asked.

"Well I suppose there is no harm in telling you now. I am taking you to a friend of Paul's. He has a house in Brixton and Paul has done a deal with him."

A deal?" I queried.

"Yes you stupid girl. He is going to buy you. They have already agreed a price, provided you come up to Paul's description of you and from what I can see you do."

I gulped, "But Madam what is he going to do with me?"

"Well I don't know girl, do I? I told you he has a house. You know?"

I must have looked blank.

"A brothel you silly girl. So what do you think he is going to do with you?"

"Oh Madam he's not going to make me work as a whore. Is he?"

She laughed, "I think that's very likely. He has a lot of kinky clients, nice well-hung black men who like fucking white Nancy boys. Paul tells me you are quite a good fuck. No doubt with training you will get even better."

"Oh please Madam, don't sell me. Can't you keep me as a maid? I'll be your slave. You won't have to pay me."

She laughed again, "I already have Jane. She's my slave, she's trained and I'm a lesbian so I don't need you. No you make up your mind to the fact that you're going to get lots of cock and make lots of money for your new Master for the next few years."

"But what do you get out of it Madam."

"Oh I've got your passport, that is worth money, and your bank books. You've got a few quid in there which should not be too difficult to get hold of."

We parked in a multi-story car park and I had another embarrassing walk through the market with people staring at me. When we got to the house Paul's friend was expecting us. I was stripped naked and he examined me like you would a horse and then he pronounced himself satisfied. The last I saw of Mrs Johnson was her having a drink with my new owner, as I was lead away in a collar and lead by one of his men.

"So you really were a slave then." I said.

She smiled, "Oh yes. William wasn't too bad. As long as you did as you were told and pleased the customer he was not unkind and you got well looked after."

"William? Wasn't that what Winston's Dad was called?"

"That's right. Winston felt that London was getting too crowded and I was getting too old to be a whore. So when he opened this place he offered to buy me from his Dad to use as a skivvy. He got me quite cheap and now I'm a toilet cleaner."

"Do you enjoy that?"

"It very relaxing and sometimes a client needs help and the regulars know they can use me any way they like, so sometimes I get some fun."

At that moment there was a bump and the lift started down. We got up, the doors opened and we went our separate ways.

I am still thinking about going back up there for a part of my summer holidays. I know Winston will let me work in the kitchen and, if I'm lucky, in the toilets as well but will I get away again after? Who knows?"

Academy Incorporated

- turning fantasy into reality -

Does a reform school where adult boys, girls and special girls relive or rewrite their schooldays appeal? Or maid training for work with us at Muir Academy or as historical role-play with real spanking and bondage, or elsewhere? Or would you like to be a Master, Mistress, slave, human pony or puppy in that village? Or do you want mail-order books, magazines, implements, audio and video tapes, adult-size school or maid uniform?

We help one and all to do such things, men and women, 18 to 80s, married, couple or single; cross-dressers, transsexuals, heterosexuals, bisexuals, homosexuals, Dominants, switches, submissives, the short, tall, fat or thin, beginner or those who've done it all, able- bodied or otherwise, any race or religion. Discreetly too, and in safety, since 1987.

For free info.

contact:

PO Box 135, Hereford, HR2 7WL, UK

www.tawse.co, email: guy@tawse.co

or ring 01432 343100

Lightning Source UK Ltd.
Milton Keynes UK
UKHW011913050122
396669UK00003B/39